TRACING YOUR ARISTOCRATIC ANCESTORS

FAMILY HISTORY FROM PEN & SWORD

How Your Ancestors Lived

TRACING YOUR ARISTOCRATIC ANCESTORS

A Guide for Family Historians

Anthony Adolph

Pen & Sword

FAMILY HISTORY

First published in Great Britain in 2013 by
PEN & SWORD FAMILY HISTORY
An imprint of
Pen & Sword Books Ltd
47 Church Street
Barnsley
South Yorkshire
S70 2AS

ISBN 978-1-78159-164-2

A CIP catalogue record for this book is available from the British Library.

Typeset by Concept, Huddersfield, West Yorkshire.
Printed and bound in England by CPI Group (UK) Ltd, Croydon, CR0 4YY.

Pen & Sword Books Ltd incorporates the imprints of
Pen & Sword Aviation, Pen & Sword Family History, Pen & Sword Maritime,
Pen & Sword Military, Pen & Sword Discovery, Wharncliffe Local History,
Wharncliffe True Crime, Wharncliffe Transport, Pen & Sword Select,
Pen & Sword Military Classics, Leo Cooper, The Praetorian Press,
Remember When, Seaforth Publishing and Frontline Publishing.

For a complete list of Pen & Sword titles please contact
PEN & SWORD BOOKS LIMITED
47 Church Street, Barnsley, South Yorkshire, S70 2AS, England
E-mail: enquiries@pen-and-sword.co.uk
Website: www.pen-and-sword.co.uk

CONTENTS

To Ann Rietchel, my aunt and godmother,
who did so much to encourage me to read
and to enjoy the world of books.

INTRODUCTION

I would have you know, Sancho, that there are two kinds of lineages in the world: those which trace their descent from princes and monarchs, and which little by little time has diminished and reduced to a point like a pyramid upside down: and others which derive their origin from common folk, and climb step by step till they achieve the dignity of great lords. So that the difference is between those who were and are no longer, and those who are but once were not. It is possible that I may prove to be one of the former, and that, on enquiry, my descent may prove great and noble ...

So said Don Quixote, in the words of his seventeenth-century creator, Miguel de Cervantes. Although we tend not to think of Don Quixote as an aspiring amateur genealogist, he was evidently very keen to discover his aristocratic ancestry.

Very little has changed over the four centuries since Cervantes lived. When it became apparent that Kate Middleton was likely to marry Prince William of Wales, genealogists and journalists went into a flurry of activity to trace her roots. What they wanted most was to link her back to aristocratic forebears, who might open the gateway to that Holy Grail of genealogy – royal blood.

As a professional genealogist, I hear regularly from people with stories of aristocratic and royal connections. It is one of the chief reasons why people start investigating their ancestry. It may well be why you are reading this now.

It is a desire I understand very well from my own experience. I grew up with several family stories about aristocratic ancestors. Assuming they were true, I enjoyed exploring all the illustrious connections with which these provided me.

One descent purported to go back to the Dukes of Somerset, and came with a detailed pedigree to prove it. Aged 14 and entirely ignorant of how to go about such matters, I wrote to the present duke, who very kindly directed me 'to a copy of *Burke's Peerage*, which you should find in your local library. Good hunting!'

A lot of hunting ensued. I found *Burke's*, alright, and plunged for the first time into its densely printed narrative pedigrees, eagerly waiting for my connection to appear. It didn't. Eventually, I came to the crushing conclusion that the pedigree I had inherited was wrong, the product of an over-active nineteenth-century imagination.

Later, however, tracing back up another part of the same side of the family, I came to a family who really were listed in *Burke's Landed Gentry*. Some of their wives were daughters of baronets, some of whom in turn had married daughters of barons, whose pedigrees were in *Burke's Peerage*. On I went, back in time, and ever higher up the social scale, past the dukes until, one fine day, I found a genuine descent from the Blessed Margaret Pole, the last of the Plantagenets, and a great-great-great-granddaughter of Edward III.

It just goes to show: the more you persist, the more likely you are to find what you want.

For me, Margaret Pole became not an end, but a beginning. She was one of Cervantes' points 'like a pyramid upside down'. Tracing back

The Blessed Margaret Pole, a truly aristocratic ancestor, whose own bloodlines lead back quickly to royalty.

through her four grandparents and eight great-grandparents led back to a glittering array of Plantagenet kings and foreign royals, and English aristocrats and Welsh dynasts. Going back even further, Margaret's ancestry led me into the realm where reality merges with myth, to Arthur, Adam and Eve, and even to the goddess Aphrodite.

Royal blood was as much a curse as a blessing for Margaret Pole. Her cousin Henry VIII identified her and her sons as potential rivals to his throne, and persecuted them relentlessly. Aged 70, she was imprisoned in the Tower, and then dragged to the executioner's block, screaming in protest. It took ten axe-strokes to end her misery.

I am only one of millions of people around the world descended from Margaret, or from other 'Gateway Ancestors', who were similar conduits through which aristocratic blood flows down from the past to the present. Most American presidents, from Washington to the Bushes, have such ancestral lines. I hope that, with the help of this book, you will soon find a line or two for yourself too.

I hope, also, that you will enjoy this book as a journey of exploration into a question that has fascinated me all my life. What is it about aristocratic ancestry that exercises such a very powerful attraction on so many people, from Don Quixote to you and me, and lures us so seductively into the fascinating pastime of tracing our family trees?

In many ways, this book picks up where the work of Sir Anthony Wagner and Sir Iain Moncrieffe left off, two generations ago: and their work stood very firmly in the tradition of the founder of our subject, the ancient Greek genealogist Hesiod. To them, and all my predecessors, I am most grateful. I have been thinking about and studying the tracing of aristocratic, royal and godly ancestors for the last twenty years, so I owe considerable gratitude to Simon Fowler for suggesting I should write 'something on researching the aristocracy and the landed gentry' for Pen & Sword. I am also deeply indebted to Rupert Harding of Pen & Sword for publishing this. Finally, I acknowledge a considerable debt to John D. McLaughlin (http:// clanmaclochlainn.com/) for first putting me onto the idea that Ireland's Milesian legends had their origins in the voyages of Aeneas. And now – to work!

Note on Websites
Some of the web addresses I wanted to cite in this book were extremely long, so I have shortened them using www.tinyurl.com. Type in the 'tinyurl' addresses I have given and your web browser will take you straight to the correct page of the correct website.

Chapter 1

A NOTE ABOUT FAMILY TREES

Since at least the start of farming, 10,000 years ago, people have remembered the names of their ancestors and recited them orally. Once we had invented kingship, we remembered lists of our kings too. When writing was invented about 5,000 years ago by the earliest urban civilisation, Mesopotamia (modern Iraq), King Lists were amongst the first things to be written down.

An obelisk erected about 4,260 years ago by the Mesopotamian king Manishtushu concerns his purchase of land that was owned in shares by descendants of the original landowner. The king had to buy it from a number of interrelated people, and he went to some pains to record this. The obelisk thus lists, in prose, different lines of descent from Push-rabī, '*ensi* [lord] of Ki.utu'. I believe it is the earliest recorded genealogy in the world.

As civilisation developed, so too did genealogies, in the same messy and disorganised fashion as the growth of our cities. The first attempt to sort them out was made by a Greek, Hesiod, who lived in Askra, not far from Delphi, about the 700s BC. He strove to seek some pattern and sense in a whirling mass of semi-contradictory writings and recitations, and is the seldom-acknowledged Father of Genealogy: the term itself is Greek, *genea logos*, 'knowledge of generations'.

Hesiod's *Theogony*, conceived whilst musing on the slopes of Mount Helicon, attempted to create an ordered genealogy of the gods, starting at the beginning – with the birth of Mother Earth – and then working logically down the different lines that sprang from her children, particularly the Titans, and their own offspring, the Olympian gods. As all families of any consequence claimed descent from the union of a mortal human with a god, Hesiod's work served to create a great umbrella from which all later human genealogies could be brought down.

All Greek genealogy was recorded in prose or poem: as Aeneas, that archetype of all aristocrats, tells Achilles in book twenty of Homer's

Iliad, 'Erichthonius sired Tros, a lord of the Trojans, and Tros, in turn, had three distinguished sons: Ilus, Assaracus and Ganymede radiant as a god ...', and so on. But due to their poetic style, and lack of any sort of visual representation, these genealogies were, understandably, rather confusing.

When Roman patricians (aristocrats) died, wax masks called *jus imagines* were made of their faces. At funerals, the family put on the masks of the dead, and recited their deeds. For the rest of the time, the masks hung on the walls of their *atriums*, just as we hang up family portraits. Sometimes they linked them together using ribbons to create *stemmae*, which were effectively family trees – but it never occurred to the Romans to record their pedigrees in a similar fashion, by drawing charts.

The technique of drawing genealogies on paper started in Dark Age Europe with boxy diagrams called *Arbor Iurii*. These showed a hypothetical family and illustrated degrees of close relations amongst which marriage was forbidden. Other early, drawn genealogies were 'Jesse Trees', illustrating the genealogy of Christ: usually, Jesse lies sleeping below, and above him ascends a series of boxes, or tree stems, each with the face of a descendant, until we reach a picture of Jesus at the top. But these were not half as tree-like as the work of medieval Arab genealogists, who drew beautiful lines of names, branching off from each other in a shrub-like style.

These really do look like branching trees, mainly because the branching growth of plants, and the branching reproduction of humans, are fuelled by the same, basic laws of nature. In *Mere Christianity* (1952), C.S. Lewis wrote that each of us seems like a separate individual because we can see ourselves only at one point in time,

> If we could see the past', he wrote, 'then of course it would look different. For there was a time when every man was part of his mother, and (earlier still) part of his father as well ... If you could see humanity spread out in time, as God sees it, it would look ... like one single growing thing – rather like a very complicated tree. Every individual would appear connected with every other.

The first true 'family trees', in which names were connected by leafy branches, were created by the Italian humanist and poet Giovanni Boccaccio (1313–75) for his *Genealogia deorum*. His 'trees' illustrated the genealogical relationships of the Greek gods and heroes, pedigrees straight out of the world of Hesiod himself. Boccaccio's charts, and those that followed, usually put the ancestor in a circle, connecting him to his offspring by lines radiating out from him. The result looked rather like the footprints left by cranes' feet in soft mud, and as a result these 'trees' gained the name 'crane's foot', which in Old French is *pied de grue,* hence the word 'pedigree'.

Hesiod, the father of genealogy, commemorated in his home town of Askra in Greece.

Until the sixteenth century, the English and Welsh heralds still tended to record genealogies in prose style, but thereafter they started using a modified form of Boccaccio's idea. They realised it was clearer to put the earliest ancestor at the top and, instead of branch-like curves, to use straight lines. The 'parent' line goes down from the parents to a horizontal, 'sibling' line, below which are written all the children, connected to the 'sibling' line by 'offspring lines'. The names of these hitherto anonymous lines were suggested to me by Princess Maria Sviatopolk-Mirski, and they seem such a good idea that I suggest we should all start using them.

It was from the heralds' decision to draw family trees using straight lines that the modern 'drop-line' family tree, or pedigree, was born.

Chapter 2

THE LIKELIHOOD OF FINDING AN ARISTOCRATIC ANCESTOR

There Must be an Aristocrat there Somewhere

If you have any British ancestry at all, then it is virtually impossible for you not to have at least a small dose of aristocratic blood.

We each have two parents, four grandparents, eight great-grandparents, sixteen great-great-grandparents and so on. If you are fortunate, and are able to trace far enough back up sufficient lines, you are almost certain to find an aristocrat.

It is possible to make such a sweeping statement on several grounds.

First is a matter of pure mathematics. 'King Solomon lived one hundred generations ago, and his line may be extinct', wrote the geneticist Sir Ronald Fisher to Charles Darwin's son Leonard in 1929: 'if not, I wager he is in the ancestry of all of us, and in nearly equal proportions, however unequally his wisdom may be distributed'.

Working back through your own family tree, the number of ancestors doubles at each generation. Just going back to AD 1200, we each have over 33 million ancestors. The population of Britain in 1200, however, was only about 2 million, with perhaps 50 million people in Europe and Africa, 250 million in Asia and much smaller numbers in the Americas and Australasia.

The figures do not add up because we are all terribly inbred. Each time two cousins marry, they reduce the total number of individuals from whom we are descended. When two first-cousins marry, their child will still have four grandparents, but only six great-grandparents. Numerous such cousin-marriages over the centuries have resulted in today's enormous population all having come from a vastly smaller population, only a millennium ago.

If families remained strictly endogamous – marrying amongst themselves, as the Ptolemies of Egypt did – our ancestries would be

Mongols sweeping across Asia: their genetic legacy accounts for about a twelfth of all men living across Asia today.

terribly limited and boring. But each time someone broke the mould and married outside their own kin-group, they brought in a dose of fresh ancestors for their descendants. This, multiplied up over the centuries, provides each of us with a stunning array of forebears, not only in this country but all over the world.

In 1999, Joseph T. Chang, a statistician at the University of Yale, wrote an influential paper called 'Recent Common Ancestors of All Present-Day Individuals' (*Advances in Applied Probability*, Vol. 31, No. 4 (Dec, 1999), pp. 1002–26). Through a complex series of equations, Chang concluded that anyone alive in AD 1200 who has any living descendants today must in fact be the ancestor of *everyone* now living. His paper caused quite a stir. Maybe he was correct statistically, but could the blood of an Australian Aboriginal in AD 1200 really have reached western Ireland now, and vice versa? It does not take much population movement to make the answer 'yes', but it still seems rather unlikely. Conservative estimates push the date back from 1200, but only as far as AD 300.

Whatever the truth is, the overall point is clear, and on a more local level it is easier to grasp. Any peasant living in Dark Age Britain, whose progeny did not die out, is likely to be the ancestor of everyone now, who has British ancestry. And by the same token, if any Dark Age aristocrat or king left progeny that did not die out, then they are

King John (1167–1216), who statistically is likely to be the ancestor of everyone of British descent living today.

likely to be our ancestors as well. Based on Chang's statistics, it is highly likely that anyone with British ancestry is descended from King John (d. 1216), all his nobles and most of his subjects too.

How Aristocratic Blood Filters Down

Naturally, there were many more peasants than aristocrats, but recent studies of genetics, together with sociological studies of human society and the evidence of many family trees, tells us much about how families developed. Most parts of the world are dominated by

10

specific male-line genetic signatures. In seventeenth-century England, the vast numbers who died of plague included hardly any aristocrats. In Scotland and Ireland, most clans can be traced back to named, aristocratic founders who lived only about a thousand years ago.

The repeated lessons of history are that one strong man and his sons can rapidly take over and dominate a wide area. He might have been a warlord who bludgeoned his way to the top, or an urbane aristocrat appointed by a higher power. Either way, so long as he produced sufficient offspring, his genes would rapidly become dominant in his locality. His descendants would favour their kin over others. They would be wealthier, better nourished, better defended, better able to take what they wanted – and better able to have liaisons with women, or rape them, than men from other families.

The pattern is the same, across the world. Genghis Khan rampaged across Asia, leaving behind a male-line genetic signature that accounts for 8 per cent of the male-line genes of all men right across Asia. In 1295, the northern English aristocrat Walter Fitz-Gilbert of Hameldone settled in Lanarkshire and spawned the extensive family of Hamilton. His descendants are now two-a-penny around Glasgow.

Younger Sons

There is an aura around aristocrats, similar to that which hallows film stars, and which pertained originally to the Greek heroes. We know they are human, yet their elevated status makes it difficult for us to imagine them interacting with the normal world in the same humdrum manner as ourselves. Winston Churchill commented after his elevation to the Order of the Garter that he would still look the same in the bath: yet the idea of anyone so exalted actually *needing* to wash seems rather unreal.

It is for this reason that the idea of aristocratic blood flowing through normal families seems so unlikely or impossible. Aristocrats inhabited another sphere altogether, so surely their blood could never have intermixed with that of ordinary folk! And if an ordinary family had noble blood, surely it would shine out so much that they would be absorbed back into the cloud of aristocracy, and regain their detachment from the mundane world about them.

Of course, it is not so, nor ever was: throughout history aristocratic families have interacted closely with the real world. Even the Queen, after all, was once filmed doing the washing-up.

It is true that aristocrats tended, as a class, to practise endogamy, marrying within their own social group. But in England, and the other parts of the British Isles that England has dominated, families have also usually practised primogeniture, by which the eldest son inherits the estate undivided. Younger siblings were usually provided for, but their incomes were from estates still in the hands of the eldest son and heir.

Younger sons tended to be farmed off into the clergy or army, so immediately dropped down a rung into the class termed the 'gentry'. Their children would marry into other clerical or military families. Their younger sons might be apprenticed into trades: tradesmen's younger sons might well find themselves labouring.

In some cases, there were labourers on aristocratic estates who were little more than third of fourth cousins of the illustrious lord who swept past them in his carriage. More often than not, however, the careers of the intervening generations took them miles, if not whole counties, away – thus avoiding too much embarrassment.

In Highland Scotland, as in Gaelic Ireland until the English system took over, and before the Conquest in the whole of the British Isles, the prevalent social system was that of clans. In the Scottish Highlands, each clan chief or laird was related to all the farmers and peasants around him, and everyone knew it. His close male-line kin were tacksmen, holders of 'tacks' or leases of reasonable-sized tracts of the clan's lands. The tacksmen tenanted these with their own junior kindred – who were in turn slightly more distant relatives of the laird. The junior offspring of the tenants were the peasant labourers. Each family knew their genealogy back to the chief's family, and bore his surname: he was the chief of the name, and in times of war, his extended family of tenants and sub-tenants provided the manpower for his personal army.

Therefore, possession of the surname of an aristocrat can well indicate that the family concerned is a junior branch of a noble line. In Highland Scotland, as also in Ireland, it is a virtual certainty.

Productive Liaisons

The gilded veil between the aristocracy and ordinary families was peppered with holes where individuals set aside class differences to indulge in carnal passion.

There must have been plenty of aristocratic wives and daughters who slept with non-noble young men, and produced children whose maternal blue blood was intermingled with the paternal genes of peasants. Nowadays, DNA tests can show such affairs up, often many centuries after they took place. But the risks were enormous – disgrace for the woman, and exile or worse for the man, and the threat of this must have been sufficient to nip a lot of ardour in the bud. But for aristocratic men, especially young ones, there was very little to put them off sleeping with women of lower classes, and often they had no need even to be discrete about it.

As well-fed, elegantly dressed, wealthy young men, they were in many ways more attractive to non-noble women than the down-at-heel men of the lower classes. They had often the power to take what they wanted, even if the women or their families did object. Even the most enraged husband might not dare exact revenge on an aristocrat who had slept with his wife. Yet often, one's wife having a child by the local lord could even be advantageous, resulting in some small financial support, or perhaps a better job or tenancy for the cuckolded husband, whose job it was to support both his wife and her baby.

Many families have stories of ancestors who were born as a result of a liaison between an aristocrat and someone of a lower class, and there are many reasons why a lot of these stories may well be true. In fact, there are probably a great many families who don't have such stories, but who are in fact descended from such liaisons anyway.

What Difference Will it Make?

The dream is that, the day you discover your aristocratic blood, a carriage will appear at the door, and a uniformed courtier will step down, salute you and lay at your feet the great wealth, prestige and power that is rightfully yours. How many people haven't daydreamed about that? Many people who start tracing their family trees protest, loudly, that they have no interest in finding aristocratic blood. I don't believe them.

To have aristocratic blood can mean everything, or nothing. There are cases when estates and titles have become vacant, and poor relations have discovered and proved their eligibility to inherit, and have been elevated to great glory. There used to be countries, such as Poland and France, where titles passed down all the male lines of families: the sons and male-line grandsons (and so on) of the original count would all be counts, and their noble status conferred on them certain privileges, such as the right to vote, or to be exempt from taxation or restrictive laws. In such instances, discovering and proving aristocratic blood could confer real benefits on the people concerned. But war and revolution has swept all such systems away.

In Britain, under primogeniture, the only beneficiaries of aristocratic blood are likely to be the senior heirs. For the rest, the first, second, third and yet more distant cousins of aristocrats, the most that is likely to be gained is a little social kudos, and perhaps the right to use the family coat of arms. But actually, there is another and very real benefit to discovering an aristocratic connection: a fantastic, ready traced family history that might stretch back centuries. That is the real prize in this game, and for genealogists and family historians, aristocratic genealogies are a rich and wonderful goal, for which it is very well worth striving.

The Mountenay Connection

Some years ago I traced the ancestry of London banker Simon Mountenay, and found that his ancestors were labourers in Nottinghamshire, descended from Benjamin Mountenay, baptised in Quorndon, Leicestershire in 1711, son of an earlier, poor weaver called Benjamin. I could not find his baptism there, or locally, but the Quorndon parish chest material (in Leicestershire Record Office) included a settlement certificate, which he had handed in when he arrived there, stating that his place of legal settlement was Atherstone in Warwickshire.

Atherstone was a hamlet in the parish of Mancetter, the registers of which show Benjamin's baptism in 1680, the fifth son of Thomas Mounteney. On investigating Mountenays in the area, I realised that there was a landed gentry family of Mountney living nearby at Newbold Verdon, Leicestershire. Their pedigree is in John Nichols' *History and Antiquities of Leicestershire*, and here Thomas appears as the third son of George Mountney Esquire, of Newbold Verdon, Leicestershire, whose father's coat of arms was recorded when the heralds visited Leicestershire in 1619. Benjamin may have been a landed gentleman's grandson, but he was the fifth son of the third son, and clearly there had not been enough money to go around, which is why his family had sunk down quickly.

Simon was able to prove his right to bear the ancient arms of Mountney, and I gained a splendid example of how some families of labourers really do have blue blood in their veins.

Chapter 3

FALSE STARTS

Why Family Stories Arise

Paradoxically, whilst most families have at least a small dose of aristocratic blood in their veins, many family stories laying specific claim to blue blood turn out to be wrong.

This is because many of the real connections that link ordinary families to noble origins tend to have been covered up very successfully, or were of such a mundane or disappointing nature that they were not remembered in stories. If someone's mother really was the victim of a duke's sexual advances, or your blue-blooded grandfather was such a lazy drunk that he ended up in the workhouse, you are not likely to want to talk about it.

On the other hand, we humans have an in-built compulsion to mythologise the past; to live vicariously through the imagined grandeur of their lives; to inspire ourselves with confidence by fantasising about noble forebears we never really had.

To tell your grandchildren that your own grandparents were unsuccessful labourers who never even attempted to raise themselves up out of the dismal rut of their boring lives does little credit to them, sheds no particularly warm light on yourself and is hardly likely to inspire your descendants to achieve anything for themselves.

The natural impulse is to euphemise the story. Nowadays, people tend to be honest about the social circumstances of their family's past, but with heavy use of euphemism: 'they led very hard lives, but they still succeeded in bringing up ten children and making sure they all went to school', or similar. Such stories may be totally untrue: the parents concerned may have been lazy and violent, and the children's schooling may have been forced on them by the parish.

But a generation or two ago – and the practice has certainly not died out – people tended to be less honest about their family's real circumstances, and when they euphemised they bunked up their ancestors' social status. To explain why the family ended up as poor as it really was, there were a number of stock stories: Grandpa had been the result of a union between a prince and a pauper, but it had to

Myself and my cousin Elizabeth English at Lambeth Palace, London, encountering our ancestral great uncle, Cardinal Reginald Pole (1500–58), the last Catholic Archbishop of Canterbury. We had been invited to Lambeth Palace to be given cuttings from the magnificent old fig tree there, grown from a cutting from the original tree brought there from Rome by Pole himself – a real 'family tree'!

be covered up; Grandpa's father was the son of an aristocrat, but he was cut off 'without a penny' by his nasty family and he was forced to become a labourer; Grandpa's mother was an aristocrat who had run off with the footman, and been disinherited; Grandpa's family were very wealthy but his father lost it through drink/gambling/the misfortunes of law/war/revolution/natural disaster. It was never, ever Grandpa's fault.

Looking Up to their Betters

We live in a heavily democratised society which has been affected deeply by socialism. We family historians are often faced with a mental leap to try to recapture the mindsets even of our grandparents' generation, let alone those of earlier ancestors, many of whom thought quite differently to us.

To most of our ancestors, the aristocracy was viewed with the awe and envy we reserve for A-list celebrities, only without the prurient cynicism, and with the additional belief that it was not just fortune, but God, who had favoured and maintained them in their privileged position. The aristocracy was the usually unattainable pinnacle to which most people aspired. In our ancestors' imaginations, to join the ranks of the aristocracy was somewhat akin to emulating the saints, whose souls were hallowed in Heaven, or the heroes of old, such as Hercules, whose spirit rose up from his pyre on Mount Iti to join the ranks of the classical gods on Mount Olympus.

Making up family stories about recent aristocratic ancestry was often the result of dearly held daydreams, and stemmed from a profound respect for the recent ancestors who were transformed into the illegitimate children of nobles, coupled with a desperate desire for self-improvement. It would be interesting to conduct a sociological study to see whether families with untrue yet persistent stories about aristocratic forebears had been sufficiently inspired to achieve genuine improvements in their social and economic conditions. Made-up aristocratic ancestors can be extremely beneficial if they inspire you to work hard at school and find a lucrative job.

In the stratified, class-ridden society of our recent forebears, anyone who wanted to succeed aspired to join a higher social class. By aspiring, they emulated, and by emulating they made themselves suitable for jobs and marriages a little further up the social ladder. If you wanted to become a station master, you adopted the bearing and conduct of an army officer. If you wanted to become a wealthy merchant, you put a fake coat of arms on your calling card, dropped hints about lordly links and behaved as if you were an earl. The social level to which you were aspiring might, on the one hand, laugh into their laced sleeves at your social pretensions, but by the same token they recognised that you were struggling towards a worthy goal, just as they were: sooner or later, once you had become rich enough, they would give in and allow you grudging admittance to their circle.

By pretending to have aristocratic ancestry, families did not set out to deceive their genealogist-descendants. They simply sought to advance themselves up the social and economic ladder, and in many cases they were modestly successful.

The False Trail of the Collingwoods

My father told me this, so it must be true. He had it from his father, so it must be ever truer.

If you are a bad or lazy researcher, you will try to prove a theory by citing multiple endorsements of your idea. If the same fact appears in three books, or on five websites, then it seems truer than if it appears only once. The fact that each secondary source may simply be repeating the same falsity does not enter your head, or if it does you will brush it aside.

When a family story has been repeated by several generations of the family, and is therefore known and repeated in several branches of the same family, it can gain the overwhelming semblance of truth. Great-grandfather, with his hoary beard, acquires the authority of an Old Testament patriarch: if he said his family were descended from the Dukes of Fantasia, then it must be true.

My mother's father was a Freeman of the City of London who never appeared in public without a tie. He told me that we were descended from Admiral Lord Collingwood, who had been Nelson's second-in-command at the Battle of Trafalgar in 1805. He believed the story implicitly, because his mother had told him. His middle name was Collingwood, and he had given the middle name to all his children on the strength of the story.

But his mother was a dreamer, who so disliked the idea of growing old that she used to pretend that her daughter was her younger sister. She used to say 'we're descended from Lord Collingwood' without paying much attention to what 'descended' really meant, and with only the dimmest idea of when the Battle of Trafalgar took place.

Her mother in turn was Mary Ann Collingwood Paterson, who had been given the middle name Collingwood because it was her mother Isabella Collingwood's maiden name. Isabella was the daughter of Matthew Collingwood, a clock-maker from Alnwick, Northumberland, who was born in 1796. He was not Lord Collingwood's son, as he knew perfectly well.

The Collingwoods were one of the families who lived along the Anglo-Scots Borders, who until very recent times had been fiercely independent clans, intent on *reiving*, that is, raiding each other as part of protracted blood feuds. Lord Collingwood was descended from one branch of the Collingwoods. Matthew was descended from another. Whether or not Matthew knew the exact genealogy, he was aware that Lord Collingwood was a kinsman of his, and was doubtless extremely proud of the fact.

In only four generations, 'related to' became 'descended from'. It was a hard lesson for me to learn, as I gradually unpicked the story and discovered the rather more interesting truth about my recent family's psychological relationship with aristocratic ancestry. It was a truth that has stood me in very good stead when decoding such family stories ever since.

False Evidence

Unrelated facts are often pressed into service to bolster up family stories of aristocratic ancestry.

In the course of the nineteenth and early twentieth centuries, the number of free schools increased dramatically. Most working class children were given strict, but often extremely good, educations in 'the three Rs', reading, writing and arithmetic. Many then went into service, or the armed forces, and were brought into direct contact with the upper echelons of society. Frequently, children from grindingly poor, illiterate, dialect-speaking backgrounds grew up with educated handwriting, strove to speak with received pronunciation and dressed and deported themselves in imitation of the upper classes. Small wonder their descendants often assume they must have been illegitimate children of noblemen.

Families have always used royal families as templates for their choice of personal names for their children. But any boy who was given a royal name, such as Augustus, Frederick, George or Edward, can be press-ganged by his descendants into providing evidence of a family connection to royalty.

Any surname that also belonged to an aristocratic family can become a licence to claim an unrealistically close connection to the noble house concerned.

My ancestor Mary Ann Collingwood Paterson, whose middle name later gave rise to a false story that she was descended from Admiral Lord Collingwood.

Many former soldiers and sailors and their families received pensions, and many families were also the recipients of financial support from charitable bodies, or received small legacies from richer relatives, or former employers. Any instance of a family receiving money without directly working for it can be pressed into service as evidence of a trust fund, set up by the noble father to benefit his illegitimate offspring.

A remembered visit by a tall, well-dressed stranger, who may simply have been the doctor, becomes a fond recollection of a noble father, or his servant, coming to check up on the family of his illegitimate child.

Any hint of heraldry in the family is seized upon with gusto. Be it a bit of pseudo-heraldry on a solicitor's seal, or any artefact with a coat of arms on it, even if that object had simply been purchased from a junk shop, becomes firm evidence of aristocratic ancestry.

Working class people might have one photograph taken of themselves in their entire lifetimes, and when they did they wanted to look as grand as possible. When photographers' studios started appearing in the nineteenth century, they usually kept a stock of fine clothes, bits of antique furniture and backgrounds depicting pillars and inspiring scenery for this reason. Such pictures are often cited as evidence that the ancestor concerned lived a much grander life than they really did, and was therefore of aristocratic origin.

There are only so many ways a mouth, nose and eyes can arrange themselves on a Western European face. Yet any combination that even vaguely resembles the portrait of an aristocrat can become irrefutable proof of a blood connection. I was once contacted by a lady who had assembled a collection of pictures of the Queen, and was convinced she looked just the same as her, and was therefore of royal blood. But, bizarrely enough, she also had some pictures of Winston Churchill, and was convinced she resembled him, and thought she was related to him, as well!

A Sense of Perspective

Well-educated forebears, with aristocratic Christian names and surnames, who received some money from a pension or legacy, or had some contact with privileged circles, and used heraldry and dressed and looked noble: all these factors *can* be clues that will lead, through patient, painstaking research, to the discovery of real, aristocratic links. When they appear in family stories that make such claims, they can sometimes be perfectly real, genuine clues and should certainly never be dismissed out of hand.

However, in many, many, many cases, all such factors are phantoms, used by people aspiring to aristocratic forebears to bolster up a family story that is simply not true.

It is by researching and disproving family stories laying false claim to noble links that you will find your true genealogical roots. In the process, you will gain fascinating insights into the psychology of the ancestors who told such stories, and you will understand them a lot better as a result. By finding and researching back your correct ancestral lines, you may eventually be rewarded by finding a genuine and hitherto completely unexpected route back to real, blue blood.

Chapter 4

FINDING AND PROVING ARISTOCRATIC ANCESTRY

Where to Start

Let us start where most of us start, with a hint, or a story, or just an aspiration that somewhere, amongst the anonymous ranks of your untraced ancestors, there lurks one who was a cut above the rest: one with a noble demeanour, an arched nose, an air of composed authority, through whose veins flowed the blue blood of the aristocracy.

As with tracing all family history, you should start with your relatives and ask them what they know. The main things to ask about, and write down faithfully, are the full names, dates and places of birth, marriage and death, and the occupations and religious denominations of each known members of the family – and any family stories. End your interview by asking for contact details of any other relatives, and repeat the exercise with them, networking ever outwards to ever more distant cousins.

For tracing relatives, close or very distant, you can use www. genesreunited.com. You type in what you know of your family tree, and the website will tell you if anyone else on the site has the same names in their own family trees. The website links up relatives quickly and easily, and helps everyone who uses it to find more relatives, and hear more family stories.

Researching the Family Story

Perhaps your starting point is a family story. It may or may not be true, but of course you will want to start here and find the truth, one way or the other. At least a story will direct your attention to one part of your spreading family tree that could yield an aristocratic connection (though later, when you investigate other, story-less sides of your family, you may be surprised to find one of those leading back to blue blood after all).

Usually, a family story comes with four components identifying: the relevant section of your family tree; the aristocratic family to which you are supposed to be linked; the mechanism by which the connection was made; and the reasons why titles and wealth did not come down to your generation.

The story may be specific about which relative was concerned – 'Grandpa's mother was the illegitimate daughter of ...', or it may be vague – 'Grandpa's mother's family was descended from ...'. If you are unsure, you could contact cousins on that side of the family and see if they have the same story: the more distant the cousins who have the same story, the better you can hone in on the relevant ancestor through whom the supposed connection arose. Then, you can focus on learning more about that side of the family, and tracing their ancestors.

The family story may be vague about who the aristocratic ancestor was. 'A German count' or 'a member of the House of Lords' is pretty unhelpful, and gives you nowhere to start looking. But many stories will name the family: 'the Earl of Bloggs', 'Prince Frederick of Bloggs'. Naturally, it makes sense to look up the individual or family in reference books such as *Burke's Peerage*, and to try to identify within the family which of the ten earls of Bloggs lived at the right time to have been the culprit.

Sometimes, you will find what you wanted. If the family story was that your great-grandmother's mother was a daughter of Viscount Bloggs, and the connection was legitimate, the entry for the Viscounts Bloggs in *Burke's Peerage* may include the marriage, and it will only take you a little research amongst birth and marriage records to prove the connection.

Illegitimate children are seldom shown in printed pedigrees. Once you have identified the likely father (or mother) in the pedigree of the aristocratic family concerned, you will know their dates of death, and you can use these to seek their wills. Sometimes people made provision for illegitimate offspring in their wills, or at least set up trust funds for purposes unspecified in the will, but known to the trustees, and which could be the looking after of an illegitimate child. You can also seek pictures of the aristocrats concerned, to see if they resembled their supposed, illegitimate descendants. You can approach the family concerned and ask if they will consent to having a comparative DNA test with you, to prove or disprove your hunch.

The mechanism by which the connection is supposed to have arisen seldom offers much opportunity for research. Elopements,

Myself visiting Thelveton Hall, Norfolk. It was built by my great-grandmother's Havers ancestors in c. 1595. I did not grow up knowing this. It was only by tracing back her family that I found and proved a link to the printed pedigree of Havers in Burke's Landed Gentry.

illegitimacies, family fallings out and so on, which furnish the most fertile elements of family stories, are usually the least well recorded. In many cases where records would be hard to find anyway, family stories often add an extra element: 'and the family destroyed the record of the birth/marriage/legacy on purpose'.

When faced with the choice between spending a lot of time working back up your family tree and searching down from the aristocratic family to whom you are supposed to be related, you are best advised to do the former. Many people have traced painstakingly down every possible line from the supposed aristocratic ancestor, only to discover they were not descended from him at all, so all their efforts had been completely wasted.

On the other hand, time and money spent tracing back your certain ancestors is never wasted. Whatever you find out about them, whether it confirms an exciting story about them or not, is not lost because it is all relevant to your forebears.

Family stories flourish in an atmosphere of mystery. If all you know of Great-Grandmother Constanza Mariotti is her name, you can easily imagine her to have been the daughter of an Italian count. Once you have her marriage and birth records, showing her father to have been an East End ice-cream seller, you can take a more reasoned view of who she really was, and embark on the enjoyable task of tracing your real Italian ancestors.

Following up Clues

As you research your family tree back in time, and whether you are specifically pursuing a family story or not, there are some clues that will indicate whether you are going in the right direction, and which may suggest a change of direction in your research.

The most obvious clue is finding a titled ancestor mentioned in a record. If you obtain a birth or marriage record, for example, in which your ancestor is referred to as 'the Hon.' (short for 'Honourable'), Sir, Bart (short for Baronet), Lady, Lord, Baron, Viscount, Earl, Marquess (or Marquis), Duke or Prince then you will know you have reached the social level whose members were well recorded in a variety of printed sources, particularly the Burke's publications. Whilst original records will still be useful for adding details and ironing out discrepancies, the bulk of your research can now be undertaken in a good genealogical library, using printed sources.

'Gent.', short for 'Gentleman', and 'Esq.', short for 'Esquire' are problematic. Up to the mid–late 1700s, they had specific meanings. An Esquire was a gentleman who had no higher title, and was entitled to use a coat of arms, whilst 'Gent.' was used, properly, for his sons. However, 'gentleman' came to be used for a broader group of men who had private incomes, and later for any man who did not directly work for a living, or who simply felt gentlemanly. By the 1800s, any retired schoolmaster or cobbler might style himself 'Gent' and not be too widely derided. Similarly, in the 1900s, the term 'Esq.' lost its specific status completely, and tends now to be added onto the end of men's names on letters, regardless of their social or economic status.

The further back you go in time, therefore, the more likely it is that the terms 'Esq.' and 'Gent.' will indicate a line that was genuinely gentlemanly, belonging to the level below the aristocracy, and quite possibly linked to it by earlier blood.

Similarly, discovering a coat of arms in family papers, or on a wax seal on letters or wills, or a sealing ring that was used for impressing such seals, offers hope. The entire aristocracy, the landed gentry, many of the clergy, the professions and the city merchants tended to acquire and be identified by coats of arms. By identifying the arms, and looking up the family who used it in printed sources, particularly the Burke's publications, you may be led back to the right pedigree.

Coats of arms were being appropriated and misused regularly by people not entitled to them from at least the 1500s onwards, so you may not always find what you expected. If your lower middle class Thompson family was misusing the arms of the Thompsons of Floggins Court, you may spend time and money examining pedigrees of the latter before realising that your own ancestors have led you on a wild goose chase. They assumed or claimed they were related to the Thompsons of Floggins Court, so they used the same arms, but in fact they were not related to them at all. That will be a frustrating thing to discover, but at least you will have learned something of your Thompson ancestors' social pretensions.

Generally, any family misusing arms was reasonably well off anyway, and they may actually have had interesting, blue-blooded ancestry that you can trace, and of which they themselves knew nothing. Even though they did not know it, your Thompsons may actually have been distantly related to the Thompsons of Floggins Court after all!

Seeking an Aristocratic Ancestor from Scratch

Even if you have no family stories concerning aristocratic ancestors, you may desire to direct your research towards finding one.

Ancestors who simply looked or sounded aristocratic may be complete red herrings. They may have been of impeccable working class origins, but have benefited from good, parish educations, and the fine clothes they wore in their studio portrait photographs may have been rented from the photographer. Many middle-class families had sunk down from upper class origins, but many more had risen up through their own hard work, so as you trace them back you will find a progression back down the social scale.

However, it generally makes sense to investigate your better-off ancestors first, in case they belonged to the 'upper class on the way down' category, whose attire and demeanour reflected the decayed grandeur of their bloodline. In that case, as you work back up their family lines, you may find the social level rising until you emerge onto the sunny uplands of aristocratic ancestry.

Ancestors with the sort of occupations that were followed by the younger branches of aristocratic families are worth pursuing. In the countryside, younger sons of aristocrats might become yeomen farmers, owning or leasing substantial farms (whereas husbandmen were holders of smaller leases, so were less likely to be from high backgrounds – though of course younger sons of yeomen could end up as husbandmen). In the towns, younger sons of aristocrats or landed gentry might be apprenticed to merchants or even prosperous tradesmen. The clergy, law and officers in the armed forces were also traditional preserves of younger sons of aristocratic families.

Research Scenarios

You have followed back the line that was 'descended from a legitimate younger son of the Duke of Bloggs', but have traced the line right back to long before the duke's title was created, and in another part of the country. The family story was incorrect: it arose out of pure ignorance because the family's true ancestry was not known. Now you have traced your ancestors correctly, and dispelled a false story.

You have traced back the line that supposedly leads to 'an illegitimate child of the Duke of Bloggs', but have found only a long line of legitimate children, and no dukes. You have probably disproved the story, unless of course one of the supposedly legitimate generations was in fact the duke's illegitimate child, secretly fostered into your family.

Maybe you will find that a couple in one generation had actually worked for the duke – they might be in a census, say, living in the duke's house as servants. Maybe the duke mentioned the mother or father in his will and left them a small legacy, which was ostensibly for them but really for the upkeep of his illegitimate child.

Maybe the duke's will indicates that he was the child's godparent, or that the child was named after him (or both – which might all be quite innocent, but *could* indicate an illegitimate connection).

You are unlikely to be able to prove such a theory using records, but you may be able to do so using DNA.

You have traced back the line that leads to 'an illegitimate child of the Duke of Bloggs', and found an illegitimate ancestor. You could well be onto something, unless your family story was just a colourful way of explaining a far less glamorous liaison between the mother and the local milkman. Bastardy bonds exist, and often identify the fathers of illegitimate children, but genuinely high-born men were seldom humiliated in such a manner.

You have followed back the line that was 'descended from a younger son of Frederick Clemo, Duke of Bloggs', and have come to a John Clemo, who could be his younger son. If you are a bad genealogist, or pretty much any nineteenth-century researcher, you will immediately add the duke to your family tree.

If you are a good genealogist, you will try to find an alternative origin for John. Are his and his real (non-aristocratic) father's baptisms in the registers of his home parish? Were non-aristocratic Clemos there for centuries before?

If John was a farm labourer, he probably wasn't the duke's younger son. If he was an army officer, however, then he may have been of ducal extraction. Printed pedigrees such as Burke's are often quite vague about younger branches, so you could investigate these using the parish registers for their home parish, to learn more about them.

The best original source for proving connections like this are wills. You would expect John, if he was the duke's younger son, to have written one. He might say in his will that he wanted to be buried in the ducal vault, or he might leave legacies to brothers and sisters who appear in the duke's pedigree.

If your theory is right then the will of the duke himself should mention John, and may provide a clue that his John is the same as yours (maybe your John is married to a Penelope, and the duke mentions Penelope as his daughter-in-law). The wills of the duke's wife, and other children, and even members of his extended family should be examined too. There may be a marriage settlement for John to Penelope, identifying a few of his aristocratic relations.

A DNA test between yourself and a definite member of the duke's family may provide clear proof that your theory is correct.

The Gifford Connection

The precious little piece of paper seen below fell out of a bag of family memorabilia into my teenage lap many years ago, and inspired a furious amount of research. 'Angela' was my great-grandmother. I avidly followed up her connection to the Mostyn baronets using *Burke's Peerage* and, as can be seen from the extract on the page opposite, I confirmed it to be accurate.

The family were Catholics, and a link back to the family of the Catholic Giffards of Chillington, Staffordshire, seemed likely. Their pedigree starts with Osburn de Bolebec, who married Avelina, sister of Gunnora, wife of Richard I of Normandy. One line comes down to John Giffard of Madeley (d. 1763), but on the Giffards' pedigree he was just shown as having three daughters, none of whom were named. Was Barbara on my family tree one of them?

John's will may have solved the problem, or Catholic baptisms, if the right ones had survived, but I got to the bottom of the mystery by asking the heralds at the College of Arms. The Slaughters had been recorded in the Heralds' Visitations in the seventeenth century, and every couple of generations they went to the College and recorded updates of their pedigree.

One update (College of Arms D.6.14) was made and signed by Thomas, the husband of Barbara, who described her as 'Barbara youngest of the 4 Daus & coheirs of John Giffard of Madeley Esq next bother to Peter Giffard of Chillington Esq deceased by Rose Brooke … now living in London 1776'. Case solved!

Sir EDWARD was *bur* March 1775; his er son,

Sir Pyers Mostyn, 6th Bt; *b* 23 Dec 1749; *m* 1780 Barbara Slaughter (*d* 2 Oct 1815), of Ingatestone, Essex, and *d* 29 Oct 1823, leaving:

Sir Edward Mostyn, 7th Bt; High Sheriff Flints 1837; *b* 10 April 1785; *m* 1st 20 Oct 1808 Frances (*d* 25 Jan 1825), dau of Nicholas Blundell, of Crosby Hall, Lancs, and had, with other issue:

1a PYERS (Sir), **8th Bt**

2a Edward Henry, JP, DL Flints; Capt 8th Hus; *b* 14 Jan 1813; *m* 16 May 1848 Anastasia Elizabeth (*d* 23 Nov 1893), widow of Edward Joseph

Part of the Mostyn pedigree from Burke's Peerage *proving that Sir Pyers Mostyn did indeed marry Barbara Slaughter.*

Chapter 5

CLUES FROM SURNAMES

Surname Origins

Before you start researching any family line, it is worth finding the origin and meaning of the surname, how it is distributed and whether it indicates that you may have aristocratic ancestors.

Most surnames have been explained in surname dictionaries (you are best advised to avoid online databases of surname meanings: some are plain rubbish). These are the best books for Britain:

> H. Harrison, *Surnames of the United Kingdom*, 2 vols (1912–19)
> G.F. Black, *The Surnames of Scotland, their origin, meaning, and history* (1946)
> P.H. Reaney and R.M. Wilson (eds), *A Dictionary of English Surnames* (1958)
> J. Rowlands, *Welsh Family History; a guide to research* (1997).
> E. MacLysaght, *The Surnames of Ireland* (1985), *Irish Families* (1957, repr. 1985) and *More Irish Families* (1970, 2nd edn 1982)
> L. Quilliam, *Surnames of the Manks* (1989)
> G. Pawley White, *A Handbook of Cornish Surnames* (1972)

Explaining how a surname arose entails finding early references to it. By revealing where these early references were, the dictionaries help indicate where the families themselves arose – and thus from whence your ancestors are likely to have come.

Indexed, comprehensive records such as census returns and General Registration records (births, marriages and deaths) are good ways of studying the locations of surnames. MacLysaght's books are specific about origins and distribution, and contain maps. For mainland Britain, a useful online resource for surname distribution is http://gbnames.publicprofiler.org/.

Aristocratic Categories

Surnames fall into five categories: locative (from place names, such as Berkeley); topographic (from landscape where people lived, such as Wood); patronymics (from the father's personal name, like Richardson); sobriquets (nicknames, such as Armstrong) and metonymics (jobs, such as Farmer).

Many families from each category have been ennobled, but the most likely types of surname to have arisen for families who were already aristocratic are the locative and patronymic ones. Whilst some locative surnames arose simply because someone came from the place name identified, many came into being because the family owned the place concerned.

Under Barclay, for example, Reaney and Wilson's A *Dictionary of English Surnames* lists Roger de Berchelai alias de Bercleia, recorded in the Domesday Book with land in Gloucestershire and Somerset; Henry de Barcley in Derbyshire subsidy rolls in 1327, and Helewys de Berkele in Sussex subsidy rolls, also for 1327. The dictionary indicates the surname was 'from Berkeley (Glos), Berkley (Som) or Barklye in Heathfield (Sussex)'. 'De' was the Norman-French for 'of' and there is a good chance here that at least some of the Berkeleys listed were manorial lords, and not just peasant families living in those places.

By contrast, they define the surname Clapper (which is a topographic surname) as 'dweller by the clapper bridge'. If you have forebears surnamed Berkeley and Clapper, and you want to find an aristocratic ancestor, you'd be best advised to focus on the Berkeleys rather than the Clappers.

Plenty of medieval English aristocratic families used patronymic surnames, especially starting 'Fitz', which was the Norman-French for 'son of', such as FitzRobert and FitzWalter. They might then drop the 'Fitz' and become plain Roberts or Walters. However, there is no automatic guarantee that the fathers commemorated by such surnames were nobles.

Most Welsh surnames were patronymics: 'ap' was Welsh for 'son of', so 'ap Thomas' meant 'son of Thomas'. Powell was a contraction of 'ap Howell', 'son of Howell'. The system was used by lords and commoners alike, and only through the difficult task of tracing a family back will you find out whether they were aristocratic or not.

In Scotland and Ireland, patronymic surnames come into their own. 'Mac' or 'Mc' is the Gaelic for 'son of', and the Irish also used 'Ua' or 'O'', 'descendant of'. The logic here was that it took the combined force of the sons of several brothers to form a new clan or sept (a sub-clan), so their unifying factor was their common descent from the same grandfather (or earlier ancestor).

The name following the Mac or O' is the name of the ancestor: MacDonald is 'son of Donald', O'Connor is 'descendant of Connor'. Such eponymous ancestors were often of royal origin, or at least had such ancestry claimed for them.

On the other hand, some old aristocratic families had surnames from other categories, such as the Spencers and Stuarts, whose metonymic surnames betray non-aristocratic origins, as household 'dispensers' and stewards respectively.

A category of sobriquets may be misleading: Bishop, Prince, Knight, King all sound very grand, but the people who actually were bishops, princes and so on had their own surnames already. In some cases such surnames may indicate an illegitimate son of such a luminary. But mostly they arose either ironically, for someone who acted above his station, or for someone who played the part of such a person in a medieval mystery play.

Surnames of Aristocrats

In many cases, families gained titles once their surnames were already fixed. The Howards, whose surname may mean 'chief steward' or just 'hedge-warden', rose from humble origins to become lawyers, land owners and then Dukes of Norfolk.

A good way of discovering whether your surname was used by aristocrats is to look it up in the *Oxford Dictionary of National Biography* (the 2004 rewrite of the older *Dictionary of National Biography*), available in good libraries and at www.oxforddnb.com/ (you can use a British library card number to log in).

The surname dictionaries and distribution maps will then help you determine whether your surname was of single or multiple origins. Reaney and Wilson define the surname Claridge as 'from Clearhedge Wood in Waldron (Sussex)', so most Claridges are probably related to each other. But Slaughter is shown to have several possible origins, from the manorial lords of Slaughter, Gloucestershire, or from common butchers. This will give you a clear sense of perspective, before you assess the likelihood of being related to aristocrats with those surnames, and deciding how much effort to devote to investigating possible connections.

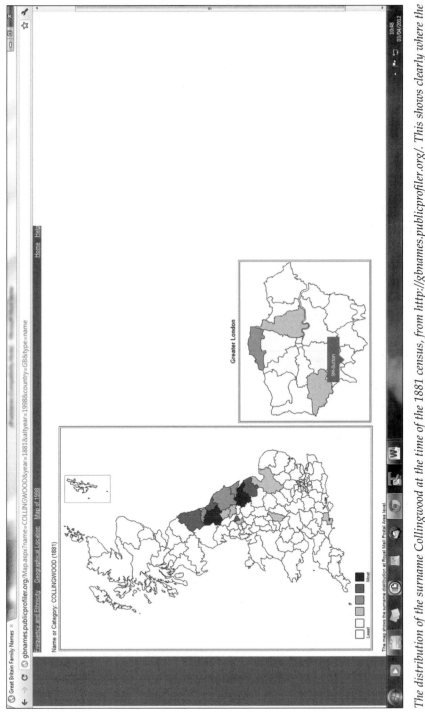

The distribution of the surname Collingwood at the time of the 1881 census, from http://gbnames.publicprofiler.org/. This shows clearly where the surname was commonest, and the areas where your Collingwood ancestors are most likely to be found.

First and Middle Names

An aristocratic surname used as a first or middle name can be a fantastic clue, unless of course such a name was simply inserted by a parent with aristocratic pretensions, or even someone who had traced their family tree and made the wrong connection.

My Hammond ancestors, who had made a completely spurious connection back to the Seymour Dukes of Somerset, actually started using Seymour as a personal name. Luckily, Seymour Hammond probably never realised his first name was based on nothing more than bad genealogy.

On the other hand, both my Havers ancestors, and their Bond and Davers cousins, made occasional use of the personal name Jermyn to commemorate their genuine descent from the Jermyns of Rushbrook. It started when the last Lord Jermyn was growing old without a male heir, and the men who had married into the family were hopeful of a sizeable inheritance for their children. Jermyn Havers and Jermyn Bond were left disappointed, but Jermyn Davers' family, coming from the eldest of the potential heiresses, hit the jackpot. The Davers' inheritance was then inherited, via a later heiress, by the Hervey family, who were then granted the title of Earl Jermyn to commemorate everything – lands, wealth and genes – which they had inherited from the Jermyn family.

But a distant cousin, the Revd Ralph William Lyonel Tollemache-Tollemache (1826–95), outdid them all. He named his eldest son Sir Lyonel Felix Carteret Eugene Tollemache, but then became more fanciful. His sixth child was named Mabel Helmingham Ethel Huntingtower Beatrice Blazonberrie Evangeline Vise de Lou de Orellana Plantagenet Toedmag Saxon and his last son was Lyunulph Cospatrick Bruce Berkeley Jermyn Tullibardine Petersham de Orellana Dysart Plantagenet.

He called another son Lyulph Ydwallo Odin Nestor Egbert Lyonel Toedmag Hugh Erchenwyne Saxon Esa Cromwell Orma Nevill Dysart Plantagenet, which is an acronym spelling out 'LYONEL THE SECOND', and James Joyce parodied this in *Finnegan's Wake*, with a character called Helmingham Erchenwyne Rutter Egbert Crumwall Odin Maximus Esme Saxon Esa Vercingetorix Ethelwulf Rupprecht Ydwalla Bentley Osmund Dysart Yggdrasselmann – whose name spells out 'HERE COMES EVERYBODY'!

On the trail of Lucretzia

If you have the name Lucretzia in your family tree, and don't know why, this story may help. In the late seventeenth century, Cornjelis Dutrij of Alost in Flanders (d. 1739) had several children including Lucretzia, who married Maximillian Josef Pije Dufayt, and Johannes (d. 1745), who settled in London as a merchant.

Johannes 'Dutry' had a daughter Catherine, who married Thomas Havers of Thelveton Hall (d. 1797). They named one of their daughters (born in 1760) Lucretzia after her maternal great-aunt, Lucretzia Dufayt (who may have been her godmother). They had another daughter Mary Havers, who married Jeremiah Norris in 1789 and had several daughters, one of whom Mary chose to name Lucretzia after her sister: whether she was also keen on commemorating the family's earlier Dutch connections as well, we do not know.

Meanwhile, the Lucretzia Havers who was born in 1760 grew up and married Thomas Wright, a banker whose bank was in Henrietta Street, Covent Garden. The Wrights had a daughter Anne who married William Charles Jerningham. The latter had several children including a son Frederick (who chose to name one of his daughters Lucretzia, after his grandmother) and a daughter, Lucretzia Jerningham. She married Edward Anthony, 13th Lord Gormanston, and proceeded to have a daughter – Lucretzia Pauline Mary (1860–1916), wife of John Arthur Farrell, DL, of Moyalty, Co. Meath.

That is just one route by which a personal name came cascading down within a family for several centuries – not by a conscious desire to keep it for its deeper historical connections, I think, but simply by each generation naming a child after a sister, aunt or grandmother.

Changes of Surname

Families of all classes changed their surnames, often quite informally, but the higher up the social ladder you go, the more likely such changes are to have been recorded.

Some did so by Royal Licence (see The National Archives' research guide 'Changes of Name' under www.nationalarchives.gov.uk/records/). Others did so by deed poll, enrolled in the High Court of Justice (in class J 18 at The National Archives; those made before 1903 are in the Close Rolls at The National Archives). From 1914 it was obligatory to publish deed polls in the *London Gazette*. Many notices were published in newspapers, particularly *The Times*. See W.P. Phillimore and E.A. Fry's *An index to changes of name under authority of act of Parliament or royal license and including irregular changes from ... 1760 to 1901* (1905, repr. 1968).

The records are useful for tracking changes made due to inheritance, or just the hope of inheritance. Sometimes you will find a middle-class family altering their surname, or adding an extra one with a hyphen, because of their belief, founded or not, in their descent from aristocratic origins.

Chapter 6

HERALDRY

'The Handmaid of History'

Heraldry is closely connected to aristocratic ancestry. You can enjoy studying the heraldry of aristocratic ancestors, and you can use it to find such forebears in the first place. Discovering a coat of arms amongst family heirlooms – on notepaper, seals, plates or glasses – or on family gravestones, can provide a fantastic clue. You can decode and identify the arms and then look for pedigrees for the family who used the arms, to see if your own, known ancestors appear.

The pitfalls are numerous. Your ancestors may just have bought an artefact with someone else's coat of arms on it, or they may have assumed someone else's coat of arms, to which they had no entitlement. In the latter case, though, all is not lost, as such an assumption will at least tell you what your forebears thought, or hoped, about their origins.

Heraldry's prehistory starts with the pictures of animals painted in the Ice Age caves of France, and scratched on the walls of caves in the Cheddar Gorge, Somerset and Creswell Crags, Derbyshire. Some of these were probably family totems. Families continued to represent themselves by use of animal symbolism down to Imperial Roman times. In the *Aeneid*, Virgil wrote of Aventinus using the same shield, showing the snaky heads of the Hydra, as his father Hercules, and described the prow of Trojan Aeneas's ship, emblazoned with two lions.

True heraldry started in the 1100s in northern France, inspired by Virgil and used first by Henry I of England, who believed he had Trojan ancestry, and who gave his son-in-law Geoffrey Plantagenet a shield depicting lions on a blue background. Later modified to a red field with three golden lions, it had become the hereditary coat of arms of the kings of England by the time of Geoffrey's grandson, Richard the Lion Heart.

Soon all knights, who had hitherto been rather anonymous behind their gleaming helmets, were adorned with shields, surcoats and crests all emblazoned with colourful and distinctive emblems which, crucially, they passed on to their sons. These 'armorial bearings' or 'coats of arms' quickly became hereditary emblems of individual, knightly families. Heralds took on the role of recording and identifying these arms, so the subject became known as 'heraldry'.

The Right to Arms

Early arms, recorded in long rolls of arms by the heralds, gained the stamp of authority through ancient usage. All later use of heraldry required royal authority, delegated down through the principal heralds, who were called the Kings of Arms, who issued grants of

The coat of arms of John Drummond, Earl of Melfort, illustrated in 1686. The earl, like many of the more distinguished sort of armigers, had supporters, in this case two lions, which stand, proudly holding up the shield.

The achievement of arms of the Forbes family, painted by leading heraldic artist Tom Meek (www.heraldicart.com). Above the coat of arms is the helm, to which the decorative mantling is attached by a strip of twisted cloth, called the torse. On top sits the crest. The motto is shown on a scroll: as this is a Scottish coat of arms, the motto is above the crest, for all others, it would usually be shown below the coat of arms.

41

new armorial bearings. Use of newly granted arms was almost always limited to the original grantee and his male-line descendants – his sons, their sons and so on. Subsequent generations were obliged to inform the heralds of their existence, so as to receive permission to continue using the arms.

That medieval system persists to this day. Nobody may use a coat of arms without the heralds' authority. There are no exceptions.

Coats of arms are not tied to a specific social rank: they are common to everyone who could fight as knights, from untitled landed proprietors up through the ranks of nobility, to kings and emperors. From the Wars of the Roses onwards, many town-based merchants and clergymen began to apply for grants of arms too, so the system thus embraced the 'upper middle class' – and those who aspired to it.

Regardless of ancestry, being entitled to use a coat of arms confers gentility upon the bearer: the only true 'gentleman', technically, is an 'armigerous' gentleman.

Of Cadency and Quarterings

Within families, individuals are supposed to be identified by marks of 'difference' or 'cadency', small emblems placed near the top of the arms. The Scots tend to use coloured borders, whilst for the rest of the British Isles you will find:

Eldest son and heir: three-pointed label (which he removes once
    his father has died)
Second son: crescent
Third son: mullet (five-pointed star)
Fourth son: martlet
Fifth son: ring
Sixth son: fleur-de-lys
Seventh son: rose
Eighth son: millrind cross

All descendants of the second son will keep the crescent: telling *them* apart involves using the same symbols again, so by the third generation the shield can become rather crowded, and the system doesn't work very well. Still, a coat of arms including the cadency mark of a martlet indicates that the bearer was (or was descended from) the fourth son of an armigerous family.

Coats of arms relate to the male line of the family. Until 1997, most ladies could use arms only by courtesy of their fathers or husbands, and usually displayed them on an oval or diamond-shaped lozenge. Since 1997, ladies have been allowed to bear arms, on shields, like men, but they cannot transmit these to their sons: that right is still restricted to men.

The left-hand side of the shield is called the 'dexter', because heralds think of it from the point of view of the man standing *behind* the shield: the right-hand side, for the same reason, is termed 'sinister'. When an armiger marries the daughter of another armiger, his shield is divided into two: his arms are squashed into the dexter side and his wife's father's are squashed into the sinister side. The wife's family arms are said to be 'impaled' by those of the husband.

If the lady concerned is the heiress (or co-heiress) of her armigerous family, then when the father dies, the husband reverts to filling the whole shield with his arms, but he places a small shield or escutcheon at the centre of it, showing his late father-in-law's arms. Once the lady herself has died, the couple's children quarter both arms, dividing their shield into four quarters, placing their father's arms in the top left (first) and bottom right (fourth) quarters, and their late maternal grandfather's in the other two (second and third) quarters. They thus show themselves to be the representatives of both families.

'Quarter' does not mean 'a fourth': it means 'living quarters', i.e., houses. If someone with a quartered coat of arms marries another heiress, then the same rigmarole applies, but with the resulting descendants showing the original male line's coat of arms in the first and fourth quarters, the first heiress's arms in the second and the more recent heiress's in the third. If a fourth quartering appears, it replaces the repetition of the original male line's arms in the fourth quarter. If more space is needed, there can be six, eight or as many quarterings as desired, and some families ended up with a great many.

Once you have identified each coat of arms on a quartered shield, you will know that the bearer was descended, *somehow*, from heiresses of each family concerned. It can take some time to research up the male and female lines to find out how each coat of arms actually came into the family.

Sometimes you will find splendid, heraldic pedigrees called 'seize quartiers', which display the arms of all sixteen great-great-grand-parents, proving that all were armigerous.

This fine coat of arms is in the chapel at Lullingstone Castle, Kent and shows fourteen quarterings with a motto below (and a lot of non-heraldic decoration around the shield).

Many aristocratic ancestors are commemorated in funeral hatchments in parish churches. These are diamond-shaped boards, showing the arms, usually, of husband impaling wife: when one partner died, the background of their half of the hatchment was painted black. When the other died, the background of the other half was painted black too. Sometimes, the job was never finished, giving the peculiar

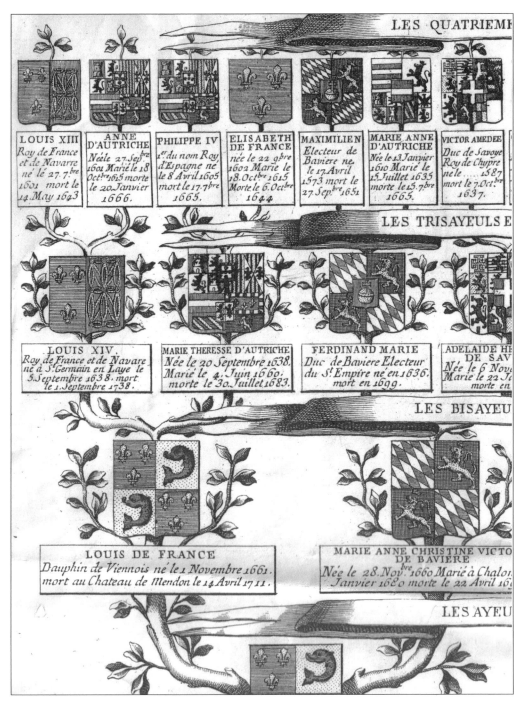

Part of the Seize Quartiers of Louis, Dauphin of France (b. 1729).

impression that one party to a seventeenth or eighteenth-century marriage is still alive! Phillimore's *Hatchments in Britain* series, 10 vols (1974–94) surveys surviving church hatchments.

Identifying Arms

Sometimes you can guess whose arms are depicted, as heralds loved puns. A shield showing bugle horns or running hounds will probably belong to Hunts, Forresters or Forsters; one showing fish may be for Fishers or Salmons, and so on.

To identify arms definitively, you must first learn how to blazon or describe a coat of arms using correct heraldic language. This is explained in specialist heraldry books such as S. Friar and J. Ferguson's *Basic Heraldry* (1993).

Having blazoned the arms, you can then look them up in an 'ordinary', a book that arranges coats of arms by their main charges (all coats with lions in them are listed together, for example). The main ordinary for Britain is J.W. Papworth and A.W. Morant, *An alphabetical dictionary of arms belonging to families of Great Britain and Ireland forming an extensive ordinary of British armorials* (1874), reprinted as *Papworth's ordinary of British armorials* (1961). If the arms are European, consult J. van Helmont's *Dictionnaire de Renesse* (1992).

There are many compilations of coats or arms, crests and mottos (to remind you, the crest is the part of the armorial bearings that sits on top of the helmet: 'crest' is *not* a synonym for a coat of arms). The best for British coats of arms is *Burke's General Armory of England, Scotland, Ireland and Wales* (1842, new edn 1884 and repr. 1961) and C.R. Humphery-Smith's *General Armory Two, Alfred Morant's additions & corrections to Burke's General Armory* (1973). These cover arms, crests and mottos.

For crests alone, that are often found on note paper, glassware and so on, you can also use *Fairbairn's crests of the families of Great Britain & Ireland* (1986), whilst mottos are identified, along with crests, in Henry Washbourne's *The Book of Family Crests* (1840). More decorative than genealogically useful is A.C. Fox-Davies's *Armorial Families* (1902), but it is still worth a browse.

For Europe, there is J.B. Rietstap's *Armorial Général* (1884, repr. 1965) with eight supplementary volumes indexed in a ninth one, and J. Siebmacher's *Wappenbüchern 1605–1961*, indexed in Hans Jäger-

A fine set of elephant and boar crests from Washbourne's The Book of Family Crests.

Sunstenau's *General-index zu den Siebmacher's Wappenbüchern 1605–1961* (1964); an almost full set of the latter is at the Institute of Heraldic and Genealogical Studies, Canterbury.

Heraldic Authorities

The use of British heraldry in still controlled by the heralds, headed by the Kings of Arms, to whom the monarch delegates their authority in this field. For England, Wales and Northern Ireland, the authority is The College of Arms, Queen Victoria Street, London, EC4V 4BT, www.collegeofarms.gov.uk. Its records include the Court of Chivalry, which heard cases concerning disputes over coats of arms. Useful printed sources include G.D. Squibb's 'Reports of heraldic cases in the court of chivalry, 1623–1732', *Harleian Society*, 107 (1956) and 'The Court of Chivalry 1634–1640', http://tinyurl.com/bracjpm.

For Scotland, the authority is The Court of the Lord Lyon King of Arms, HM New Register House, Edinburgh, Scotland, EH1 3YT, www.heraldry-scotland.co.uk/lyoncourt.htm. Scotland's Public Register of all Arms and Bearings in Scotland (1672–1902) is in Sir

The gilded gateway to the College of Arms, London.

J. Balfour Paul's *An ordinary of arms contained in the public register of all arms and bearings in Scotland* (1903) and with an extra *An ordinary of arms*, Vol. 2 (1977) up to the 1970s. The Public Register (1672–1907) is also online, at www.scotlandspeople.gov.uk.

The Republic of Ireland has its own heraldic authority, the Chief Herald of Ireland's Office, 2 Kildare Street, Dublin 2, http://tinyurl.com/93amu74, with its records housed in The Genealogical Office, part of the National Library of Ireland (at the same address).

All these authorities hold excellent genealogical records of armigerous families and can be applied to for reports thereon.

For all heraldic matters you can also consult The Heraldry Society, c/o The Secretary, PO Box 772, Guildford, Surrey, GU3 3ZX, www.theheraldrysociety.com.

To study the subject more fully, H. Stanford London's *The Right Road for the Study of Heraldry* (1968) is recommended.

Claiming a Coat of Arms

If your research proves you are descended in the male line from an armigerous family, and ultimately from a male-line ancestor to whom arms were granted, then you can apply to the heralds for permission to use the arms, with appropriate differencing. They will examine your evidence and record it as a continuation of their earlier pedigree material on the same family. The standard of proof required is extremely rigorous: if there is *any* doubt over any connections, they will send you away to find better evidence. Even a baptism in one parish followed by a marriage and children baptised in another nearby parish causes problems. How do you know for sure, they will say, that these two men are the same? It will be up to you to furnish more convincing proof – mention of the man's children in his own father's will, for example.

If Kate Middleton, now Duchess of Cambridge, had wanted to trace back to royal connections, she would have been well advised to go up the prosperous Lupton side of her father's family tree, rather than explore the humble, workaday ancestry of her mother.

As it was, the enterprising American genealogist William Addams Reitwiesner explored both on his own initiative, and found a line back from the Luptons to John Fairfax, a parchment-maker in sixteenth-century Norwich – who also happens to be an ancestor of my grandmother's. John was probably a younger brother of William Fairfax of Walsingham: William appears in the Heralds' Visitation of Norfolk, with no younger siblings shown, and nobody (including me) has ever been able to prove the connection conclusively. It is very likely, however, and if so, we can speculate on his earlier ancestry.

The heralds recorded the father of William of Walsingham (and, by implication, of John the parchment-maker) as William Fairfax 'of Suffolk', and they recognised his right to use the arms of the Fairfaxes of Walton, Yorkshire, differences by use of a martlet, which is the cadency mark for a fourth son. The Heralds' Visitations of Yorkshire show a William Fairfax as the fourth son of Sir Thomas Fairfax of Walton and his wife Anne Gascoigne, and what can be gathered of the dates of those concerned fits well. The martlet indicates that William of Suffolk was Sir Thomas and Anne's son. Unfortunately, the link cannot be proved firmly: William is mentioned in various Yorkshire Fairfax wills, but never with any indication that he was – or wasn't – living in Suffolk.

If the connections are correct, this pedigree would give Kate some wonderful genealogical links. Sir Thomas Fairfax's eldest son Nicholas was an ancestor of the late Diana, Princes of Wales. Sir Thomas's wife Anne Gascoigne was descended from Edward III. Anne's sister Elizabeth Talboys was the great-great-great-grandmother of Mildred Reade who married Colonel Augustine Washington, great-grandparents both of George Washington, first president of America and also of the Revd Robert Porteus, whose great-granddaughter Frances Smith became Countess of Strathmore and was grandmother of the late Queen Elizabeth the Queen Mother.

There is a twist to every story. Recently, Christopher Challoner Child told me that Andrew Pattison, an amateur genealogist, discovered that Kate's *mother* Carole Goldsmith was descended from Edward IV, via the Harrison family. The Harrisons were amongst the least likely of the Duchess's forebears to have had royal forebears, as they were Durham coal miners – so it just goes to show.

Edward IV had an illegitimate child, Elizabeth, wife of Thomas Lumley, whose aristocratic descendants included the Conyers baronets. However, the family's wealth was squandered away in the eighteenth century and the last, Sir Thomas Conyers, 9th baronet, was a pauper living in Chester-le-Street Workhouse. His daughter Jane and her descendants may have been blue-blooded, but in economic terms they were working class. Extraordinarily, however, the Durham genealogist Robert Surtees (1779–1834) actually predicted what might happen next: 'A time may yet come, perchance, when a descendant of one of these simple artizans may arise, not unworthy of the Conyers' ancient renown ...'. How right he was! Jane's grandson Anthony Liddle was a 3 × great-grandfather of Kate's mother Carole.

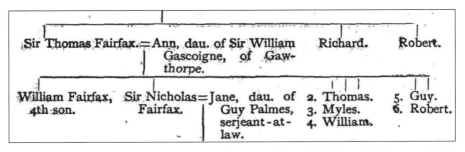

Part of the Fairfax pedigree from the Visitations of Yorkshire (1584/5 and 1612), as published by Joseph Foster in 1875. It shows Sir Thomas's fourth son William Fairfax twice, though for no obvious reason. He almost certainly settled in East Anglia and was an ancestor of Kate's father.

Chapter 7

WHO WERE THE ARISTOCRATS?

From Emperors to Princes

The Greeks spread the trappings of civilisation – city-building, writing, money and so on – throughout the western Mediterranean, and the Romans brought that culture north, planting it firmly in Gaul (France) and then, in AD 43, in Britain. When the Roman Empire collapsed at the start of the fifth century AD, the barbarians who succeed them adopted varying amounts of the old Roman way of life. The Franks who invaded Gaul became thoroughly Romanised, as did the Vikings who later settled in northern France, and became the Normans. When William, Duke of Normandy invaded England in 1066, he imposed the Normans' reinvented, Romanised civilisation upon Anglo-Saxon England.

At the top of the pile are emperors, whose title is from the Latin *imperator*, 'commander', an honourific title that Augustus Caesar arrogated to himself and his successors, back in the first century BC. The western Roman Empire was revived with papal backing in Germany under the Frankish ruler Charlemagne in AD 800, and throughout the Middle Ages England was theoretically part of this Holy Roman Empire. The idea of empire was later revived by the Prussian kings, who called themselves emperors (or kaisers, the German equivalent of 'Caesar'). Further east, the Grand Princes of Moscow, who were of Viking origin, extended their rule over Russia and claimed a continuity of imperial sanction from the eastern half of the Roman Empire, styling themselves Caesar or Czar, also spelled Tsar. Queen Victoria became Empress of India in 1876, and that title was used by British monarchs until Indian Independence in 1947.

Below the emperors are kings, rulers of individual states. Their Latin title was *rex*, which became *roi* in French. The German and Saxon equivalents were *könig* or king, derived from the Norse *konungr*, meaning 'kin of the sacred kindred', and referring to their descent from the Norse gods. The Saxon term for the king's wife, *quen*, 'queen', is from an old Indo-European root that ultimately just meant 'woman'. William the Conqueror called himself both 'Rex' and 'King', the former to emphasise his pseudo-Roman authority and the latter to remind the Saxons, in their own language, that he was in charge.

Below kings are princes, from the Latin *princeps*, used for the head of the Roman Senate, and adopted by Augustus, after which it became a royal title. 'Prince' (and the female equivalent, Princess) can be a courtesy title for immediate members of kingly families, or the title of independent or semi-rulers – the bishopric of Durham used to hold certain territorial rights over the county palatine of Durham, and these conferred the title of Prince onto the incumbent bishop. The Principality of Wales has traditionally been granted to the English monarch's heir since the time of Edward I.

The Peerage

Below kings and princes are the tiers of dukes, marquesses, earls, viscounts and barons, who are known collectively as 'the peerage', and whose chief, defining characteristic, until the reforms of New Labour, was that they sat in the House of Lords.

The term 'lord' is a catch-all term, a Saxon equivalent of the Latin *dominus*, that simply denoted 'the master'. It is occasionally used as a title in its own right, such as 'Lord of [the Isle of] Mann', and it is also the courtesy title of the younger sons of dukes and marquesses (and 'lady' for daughters). It is used when addressing peers from the ranks of barons up to marquesses, so the Marquess of Bloggs is addressed as 'Lord Bloggs'. Confusingly, 'lord' is also used for many other non-noble titles, such as lords of manors, lord mayors, lord chamberlains and so on, where the term has nothing at all to do with hereditary peerages.

'Peer' means simply 'equal' and conveys the notion that, when voting in the House of Lords, all noblemen carry equal weight.

It is the peerage that, strictly speaking, comprises our aristocracy. The term 'aristocracy' is from the Greek ἀριστοκρατία, 'the excellent [men] of the state'. The term referred initially to the leaders of the Athenian army, and was used later of military leaders throughout the classical world. Its use in Britain reminds us that the original purpose of the aristocracy was to raise armies to fight for the king, a purpose the Conqueror understood well when he parcelled out

William the Conqueror, as imagined by a nineteenth-century engraver.

his new realm amongst the knights who had accompanied him from Normandy.

The highest tier of the peerage is the dukes, from the Latin title *dux*, denoting a regional military commander. Roman Britain seems to have had at least two, one commanding Hadrian's Wall and the other guarding the 'Saxon Shore' of Kent and Sussex. Edward III revived the title, making two of his sons Duke of Cornwall and Duke of Clarence, and his cousin Henry of Grosmont Duke of Lancaster, a title re-granted after Henry's death to Edward's son John of Gaunt. During the later Middle Ages the ducal rank was broadened out to include some high-born aristocrats who were not members of the royal family. Winston Churchill was offered a dukedom as a reward for winning the Second World War, but declined it.

Below dukes are marquesses, from *mark* (or *march*), a Germanic word for a boundary, and first used by the Franks for aristocrats appointed to hold and fortify border regions. England had an Earl of March for the Welsh border region and it was only in the late 1300s, and then more formally in the 1500s, that the title marquess started to be granted to nobles, simply as a title, without any obvious connection to borders.

Below this comes the older title of earl. The original earls were Saxon chieftains subject to the Saxon kings (sometimes, these *earldormen* or *eorls* used *dux* as a Latin equivalent of their title). In France and thus in Normandy, the equivalent of earls were *comes* or counts, 'companions', referring to the warriors who formed the loyal body-guard around the military leader, but later used as a title for regional military officials appointed by the ruler. The Normans in England turned the old Saxon shires into counties by placing them under the command of counts, but they used the Saxon title earl for the men in charge of the counties, so as to command the loyalty of the Saxon populace. But earls' wives have always retained the Continental style, countess.

Below earls are viscounts, *vice-counts*, the equivalents of the Saxon shire-reeves or sheriffs, who were originally deputies of the earls or counts. 'Viscount' was first granted as peerage title to John, Viscount Beaumont in 1440.

Below viscounts are barons, from the late-Latin *baro*, for a soldier. The Normans used the term for feudal lords or tenants-in-chief, the strong-men amongst whom the Conqueror had portioned up the country, and who were summoned to attend the king in the national assembly that became known as Parliament, and later the House of Lords.

Usually, families start by being ennobled as barons, and then, if they serve the monarch well, they might be promoted upwards, to viscount, earl, marquess and eventually duke. If in particular favour, a nobleman might be promoted up by several ranks at a time, but he would usually be granted the intermediate titles anyway, so he might be promoted from baron straight up to earl, with a viscountcy thrown in for good measure. Such 'spare' titles are used as courtesy titles by the senior male heirs of the head of the family.

The English peerage system was imposed by conquest on Wales and Ireland and was introduced into Scotland by the Scots kings, who were keen to emulate the robust system of government of their Norman neighbours.

Almost all officially recognised British titles have been granted by the monarch, who is the *fons honorum*, the 'fountain of honour'. The titles were based robustly in the tenure of land (which is why each one is 'of' somewhere) and in the summoning of title-holders to Parliament.

There are a few ambiguous exceptions, where titles that existed before the Norman Conquest have survived. The Lordship of the Isle of Man is one example, which comes down from the Viking kingdom of Man. It was held for a long time by the Stanley Earls of Derby and was then legally subsumed by the Crown, but retains a peculiar status as a title which, though held by the British monarchy, was not created by it.

Once the Wars of the Roses were over, the honours system evolved. Titles retained their legislative privileges, but became less concerned with land and more with prestige at court. By the nineteenth century it was possible to have a newly created aristocrat sitting in the House of Lords alongside great magnates, but whose feudal domain extended no further than his front doorstep.

Below the peerage is a level that hovers between the peerage and the gentry – the baronets. The system was devised by James I, who invited wealthy, untitled men to become baronets, receiving a knighthood that became hereditary in the senior male line of their family, and a grant of land either in Ulster or Nova Scotia. The non-negotiable price for this 'honour' was a large cash payment, and the undertaking to settle the newly granted land with Protestant settlers.

Few men who received such offers dared refuse, and the scheme worked rather too well: the royal coffers were full, western Canada was settled with English and Scots farmers and northern Ireland gained the bulk of its Protestant population, leading to four centuries of civil conflict.

Knights

Below the baronetage comes the knightage or, more accurately (because many aristocrats and royals are also knights), the majority of knights who hold no higher title.

W.A. Shaw's *The Knights of England* (1906, online at www.the genealogist.co.uk) lists all knights from the earliest times, with date and place of knighthood, in – despite the book's title – all the British Isles.

Knights are those who have actually been knighted by the sovereign. Unlike baronetcies, their title is non-hereditary, for life only. However, it was not uncommon to find families who attended the House of Commons, and rendered other services to the monarch, at court, in local administration or on the battlefield, who received knighthoods, generation after generation.

The mounted warrior was one of the most formidable engines of war in the classical world. The Greeks called them 'horsemen', *hippeos*, and the Romans *eques*, and each had social and legal privileges and obligations. The terms for knights have a convoluted history: our medieval ancestors called them *childes*, a term that ended up being used for children, whilst the term *cniht*, that became knight, was originally used for boys or servants!

Knights are addressed as 'Sir', an abbreviated form of 'Messire', the French for 'my lord'. Knights' wives are termed, by courtesy, 'Lady'. The female equivalent of a knight is a dame, from the French version of the Latin female form of dominus ('lord').

Knights come in various types and orders, from the most illustrious Knights of the Garter downwards. Like other orders of knighthood, the Garter is a medieval creation, based on the romantic tales of Arthur and his Round Table companions. On the medieval battlefield there were two types of knight, knights bachelor, who fought in companies led by knights banneret.

In medieval England, land was granted to tenants-in-chief (those who held land direct from the Crown) in return for Knight Service or Grand Serjeantry. Knight Service meant that, in return for being granted land, you had to provide a knight to fight in the king's army. If tenants-in-chiefs' sub-tenants tenanted only part of a Knight's Fee, they would pay *scutage*, money towards the maintenance of a knight. Grand Serjeantry entailed holding land in return for performing another, specified task instead of being a knight.

'Distraint of knighthood' was a medieval law (1279) requiring anyone with an income of £40 or more to attend coronations and fight in the

royal army as a knight. It was revived by Charles I, who fined those who had done neither of those things, as an extremely unpopular way of earning money for the royal coffers. The records are available at The National Archives in LR 5/56. It is salutary to remember that two things we may think of as being thoroughly glamorous and desirable – seeing the monarch crowned and becoming a knight – were, to many country squires, a thoroughly undesirable and ruinously expensive nuisance.

The Gentry

The gentry are not aristocrats, though they tended to behave aristocratically. They mixed closely with their titled neighbours and aspired to marry into the ranks of the peerage, and indeed many worked their way up to gain titles. As far as genealogists are concerned, they are an important class because they form the most usual bridge between the common masses and the gilded elite. Once a line of ancestors has been traced back from labourers to gentry, the savvy genealogist will catch a whiff of blue blood, and be off on the chase.

Burke initially collated the pedigrees of the gentry and published them as *A History of the Commoners*, a title he chose because the gentry were not titled (though actually all non-royals are commoners, even if they are dukes). The book met with a stony reception, so he rapidly re-issued it as *History of the Landed Gentry*. It gained immense popularity and came to define a social class that had previously been rather indefinable. Loosely, the criteria for being in *Burke's Landed Gentry* was being untitled, but owning freehold land, and being manorial lords. But many families who were included actually owned very little freehold, and held most of their estates (great or small) on substantial leases from grander freeholders.

As the nineteenth century progressed, the agricultural depression struck deep, causing many old gentry families to go bankrupt, whilst simultaneously new, industrial wealth catapulted many new families up to gentry status. The *Landed Gentry* started to include ever more families whose 'of' was merely their house, rather than a rolling country estate. The gentry, after all, was a social class whose membership was not by royal appointment.

The process of self-gentrification was pursued with a vigorous ardour by many an aspiring, rising dynasty. Many families gentrified themselves simply by the way they behaved, or else were gentrified in retrospect by family stories. John Clapper, leasehold farmer of Peacock

CONSTABLE-MAXWELL, OF EVERINGHAM AND CARLAVEROCK.

MAXWELL-CONSTABLE, WILLIAM, esq. of Everingham Park, in the county of York, and CARLAVEROCK CASTLE, in Dumfriesshire, b. 25th August, 1804. Mr. Constable-Maxwell succeeded his father in 1819, and, but for the attainder of WILLIAM MAXWELL, *fifth Earl of Nithsdale*, would have inherited the BARONY OF HERRIES, of Terregles, in the peerage of Scotland.

𝔏𝔦𝔫𝔢𝔞𝔤𝔢.

This gentleman being the heir and representative of two eminent families, it will be necessary to detail lines of both, we shall therefore begin with the

FAMILY OF MAXWELL.

SIR JOHN DE MACUSWELL, (eldest son of HERBERT DE MACCUSVILLE, who flourished under MALCOLM IV. and WILLIAM I.) was sheriff of the county of Roxburghe, in 1203, and 1207. He was afterwards (15th June, 1220) one of the guarantees to the marriage contract between ALEXANDER II. and the *Princess* JOAN of England, and he assisted ham, and the family of Maxwell, of Park Hill, near Newark.

The elder son,

SIR HERBERT DE MAXESWELL sate in the parliament of Scone, (5th Feb. 1283-4), when the nobles agreed to acknowledge the "MAIDEN OF NORWAY," as Queen of Scotland. He died before the year 1300, having had three sons, namely Sir John, who predeceased him, SIR HERBERT, and ALEXANDER. His successor was his second son,

SIR HERBERT MAXWELL of Karlaverok, who was s. by his son,

SIR EUSTACE MAXWELL, the gallant defender of KARLAVEROK against the power of EDWARD I. Of this celebrated fortress there is a minute and interesting description in an old heraldic French poem, which recites the names and armorial ensigns of the knights and barons who accompanied the English monarch in 1300, in his expedition to Scotland by the western marches, then under the guardianship of Sir Eustace, as Lord Warden. Karlaverock was attacked, and at that time taken. The original of the poem alluded to is preserved in the British Museum, and the passage describing the situation and form of the castle is thus rendered by Grose:

" Karlaverok was a castle so strong that it did not fear a siege, therefore on the king's arrival it refused to surrender; it being well furnished against sudden at-

Part of a typical entry from Burke's Commoners.

Farm, might change the name of his home to become 'John Peacock Esq. of Peacock House', which the family story might elevate to 'Peacock Hall', upon which, in our imaginations, and only in our imaginations, John Peacock stops being a horny-handed farmer, and starts swanning about his estate in a bell-bottomed wig surrounded by a flotilla of liveried servants.

Plenty of men acted up to this pretension in real life – or were cajoled into doing so by their wives – and ran up such vast debts that they ended up being 'gazetted', which means having notices of their bankruptcy listed in the *London Gazette*. A cautionary rhyme in William Hone's *Table Book* for 1827 spells out beautifully this social change and its dire consequences:

> *1722*
> *Man, to the plough;*
> *Wife, to the cow;*
> *Girl, to the yarn,*
> *Boy, to the barn;*
> *And your rent will be netted.*
>
> *1822*
> *Man, Tally Ho:*
> *Wife, silk and satin;*
> *Boy, Greek and Latin,*
> *And you'll be Gazetted*

The rhyme's lessons were widely ignored. When an edition of *Burke's Landed Gentry* came out in the 1930s, a newspaper quipped that very few of the people listed in its pages could afford to buy a copy.

Bankruptcy notices also feature in *The Times*, which, along with local newspapers, often reported such cases in some detail, including inventories of the possessions of the bankrupt, pianos, silks and all, which were auctioned to raise money to pay off the bankrupt's debts. The last gasps of many gentry families are thus recorded in some detail, and can provide a useful record of their descent down into the lower orders, amongst whom their impoverished blood was destined to be disseminated.

Inheritance of Titles

Until the Life Peerages Act (1958), which created barons for life, each rank, from baronet up to duke, was hereditary: it passed down from the holder to their senior heir. The identity of that heir was determined by the terms of the original creation. Until 1322, titles were inherited by the heir general, that is, the eldest surviving son, or, failing him, the eldest surviving daughter. They are known as feudal baronies, or baronies 'in fee' or 'by writ' (that is, created and recognised by a writ of summons issued by the king to summon an ancestor to Parliament). In 1322, the creation of the Earldom of Carlisle for the first time specified the descent of the title to the male-line heirs alone. This earldom was by a new method, the issuing of Letters Patent (a document issued by the king and entered into the Patent Rolls). The same formula was used for the creation of some titles thereafter and it became the usual form of almost all creations from 1441 onwards.

Thus, most peerage titles are hereditary in the senior male line, passing from father to eldest son. If the eldest son dies without a son, the title goes to his next eldest brother, or his sons, in turn. If no male-line descendants of the original grantee can be found, but it is suspected some exist, the title is deemed to be dormant. If there simply are no heirs at all, a title is declared *extinct*.

Some titles were created with 'special remainders'. When the Barony of Bury St Edmunds was created for Henry Jermyn in 1643, for example, he had no wife or children. A special remainder was therefore included in his Letters Patent, simply as a royal favour to him, whereby if he died sonless, the title would pass to his brother Thomas, and to Thomas's male-line heirs, which is what eventually happened.

If the land pertaining to older, feudal baronies had been inherited equally by two or more sisters, the title itself was deemed to be abeyant until one or more of the co-heiresses or their heirs became extinct, leaving only one living heir who could then attempt to revive and use the title. This older system led to many claims by families who considered themselves the correct heirs of abeyant titles, and the complex legalities of this hangover from the Middle Ages has exercised lawyers ever since.

Sir T.C. Banks described these in *Baronia Anglica Concentrata: or a concentrated account of all the baronies commonly called Baronies in Fie; deriving their origin from writ of summons, and not from any specific limited creation* (1844) – in other words, baronies that might be ripe for claiming. For more details see F.B. Palmer, *Peerage Law in England* (1907) and Sir Anthony Wagner's *English Genealogy* (1960, repr. 1983). Wagner wrote that this aspect of peerage law was,

> long obscured by the lawyers' requirement that what historically had been indefinite should in retrospect be given sharp and logical definition ... by a series of decisions in individual cases

between the sixteenth and the twentieth centuries a set of rules of qualification and succession was built up with retrospective application to the interpretation of thirteenth and fourteenth century events for modern purposes.

So, each case was argued over and assessed on its own merits.

Titles from baronet up to duke existed because they were both created and recognised by the monarch, under a system established by the monarchy in the first place. It therefore follows that nobody can hold such titles without the knowledge and authority of the monarch. Claims to inherit dormant, 'extinct' or abeyant peerages are heard in the House of Lords' Select Committee for Privileges, and baronetcy cases are heard in the Privy Council. The monarch's decision, based on these bodies' findings, is final.

The Parliamentary Archives (formerly the House of Lords Record Office), Houses of Parliament, London, SW1A 0PW, www.portcullis. parliament.uk, has many volumes of peerage cases, arguing the case for the claimant of a title and presenting as much detailed evidence as possible. Not all such cases were successful, by any means. Sometimes, a petitioner already using the title he claimed might take his case to the Lords, only to be told his evidence was not watertight and that he must revert to being plain 'Mr'. Successful or not, such claims and their supporting evidences are goldmines for genealogists.

Foreign Titles

Titles granted by foreign powers are usually recognised in Britain on an informal basis: those that were acknowledged formally are included in the 1939 edition of *Burke's Peerage*.

Where a foreign power that granted titles is now defunct, so too are the titles it created, but such titles are generally still recognised out of courtesy. A family of counts who were ennobled under the French kings, or the Russian tsars, is likely to be addressed as such by our monarch, should the monarch have any cause to meet them. Her Majesty does not, however, wander about Buckingham Palace fretting over whether she has every single foreign count living in Britain on her Christmas card list.

Sometimes, titles are granted by foreign powers to British subjects. Britain has plenty of papal counts, and counts of the Holy Roman Empire. Recently, in an impromptu ceremony by the Sultan of the Moluccan island of Ternate, television presenter Kate Humble was made a princess. All such titles might be recognised out of courtesy, but none have any legal relevance in Britain.

The deposition of James II in the Glorious Revolution of 1688 created a nebulous situation: the new joint-monarchs, William and Mary, claimed James was no longer king, whilst James, living in exile in Saint-Germain-en-Laye near Paris, asserted that he jolly well was – and he and his immediate successors continued granting titles to prove it. Through not valid under British law, they were nonetheless British titles granted by princes who had good enough reason to call themselves monarchs. These titles are chronicled in the Marquis de Ruvigny's *The Jacobite Peerage* (1904, repr. 1974), whilst the genealogy of the British families who lived in exile with the Stuarts are in C.E. Lart (ed.)'s *Saint-Germain-en-Laye, The Parochial Registers; Jacobite Extracts 1689–1720*, 2 vols (1910).

There have been cases in recent decades of organisations claiming sovereign rights and then granting titles, for a fee. Of course, anybody who wishes can create titles and grant them to people, but they have no meaning beyond what the individuals concerned vest in them, and they certainly have no official or legal validity. I once saw a film clip of an investiture ceremony being carried out on a sheep ranch in the Australian outback, where the farmer had declared himself an independent ruler. It was made all the pottier by the seriousness with which the succession of 'dukes' and 'earls', all dressed in home-made cloaks, were evidently taking themselves.

There have also been pretenders claiming male-line descent from the exiled Stuarts, who have claimed the right to create new titles. No such pretenders have ever adequately proved their genealogical claims, so the titles they have granted are worthless.

The Romance of Titles

Such bizarre pantomimes take place because of the deep reverence that developed for aristocratic titles over the centuries. Most titles started off as extremely practical, workaday Roman or post-Roman job descriptions. Modern equivalents would be prime minister, major general, admiral, managing director or chief executive officer. These modern 'titles' carry a degree of social cachet, and a whiff of power, but they lack the accumulated glamour of titles such as duke and earl, which go back so far into our history, and have been associated for so long with political power, military command, the tenure of large estates and great wealth.

It is this accreted gravitas of peerage titles that helps make so many people dream of inheriting one: maybe this is what motivates you most to trace your ancestry. Even if no such title could possibly be inherited, many people are still immensely happy simply to find a title being used by one of their ancestors. Just being descended from a titled person transfers part of that age-old glamour down the centuries to you, and you can bask, vicariously, in their reflected glory. Is something you can drop, nonchalantly, into conversations, or leave for people to notice on your family tree. Did I ever mention that my great-great-great-great-grandmother was the last Viscountess Montague?

You have only to listen to how loudly and vehemently many family historians claim they are *not* interested in finding aristocratic ancestors, to appreciate quite how potent aristocratic titles really are in today's supposedly fully democratised society.

As genealogists who have painstakingly traced our ancestry far back into the past, we have earned the right to wallow in the glories and mysteries of the past that we have uncovered. But our fascination with titled, aristocratic ancestors has a rigorously practical aspect too: in the process of creating, using and inheriting aristocratic titles, aristocratic ancestors generated and left behind an awful lot of jolly good records.

Chapter 8

RECORDS OF THE NOBILITY AND GENTRY

Printed Sources

Finding and using pedigrees of noble and gentry families is tremendously easy, and enjoyable, as they are all in print. Most good libraries have collections of them, the best being the British Library, older university libraries, the Society of Genealogists in London (14 Charterhouse Buildings, Goswell Road, London, EC1M 7BA, 0207 251 8799, www.sog.org.uk) and the Institute of Heraldic and Genealogical Studies (79–82 Northgate, Canterbury, Kent, CT1 1BA, 0122 776 8664, www.ihgs.ac.uk), and there are many more.

Increasing numbers of the books are online. The free http://books. google.com/ has a growing collection, as does the pay-to-view www. ancestry.co.uk. The www.wikipedia.org/ pages about the authors of county histories and peerage works often have 'external links' to online versions of their works. The Mormons have a superb collection in Salt Lake City, Utah, America, searchable and sometimes even readable at www.familysearch.org/#form=books. The Humphrys Family Tree website at http://tinyurl.com/244ve67 has links to many peerage books that are online.

However, this is an area of genealogical research where a lot of the pleasure is in the books themselves. Exquisitely bound, gilt-edged, musty smelling and fingered by centuries-worth of people like us – to sit amongst them and search your way through their pages, eventually hitting upon the right pedigree, is one of the real joys of the job, so if you have the opportunity to visit a proper library and do your research there, do not pass it up.

The main books are the visitation pedigrees, the antiquarian county histories and the volumes of printed pedigrees, of which *Burke's Peerage* and *Landed Gentry* are the best known. There are also a host of old genealogical magazines and journals devoted to printed pedigrees, particularly *Collectanea Topographica et Genealogica, Herald and Genealogist, Miscellanea Genealogica et Heraldica*, the *Ancestor*, the *Genealogist*, the *Genealogical Magazine, Topographer and Genealogist* and others, and a vast number of privately printed books about individual families.

Genealogical Bibliographies

Finding what you want is quite simple, as most of what is available is covered by bibliographies. The main British genealogical bibliography is G.W. Marshall's *The Genealogists' Guide* (4th edn 1903, repr. 1973). It is supplemented by J.B. Whitmore's *A Genealogical Guide, an index to British pedigrees in continuation of Marshall's genealogists' guide* (repr. 1953). These catalogue the pedigrees in the printed Heralds' Visitations, Burke's and the old genealogical publications.

Covering more recently printed material are G.B. Barrow's *The Genealogists' Guide, an index to printed British pedigrees and family histories 1950–75* (1977) and T.R. Thompson's *A Catalogue of British Family Histories* (3rd edn 1980).

Stuart Raymond's *British Genealogical Library Guides* (S.A. and M.J. Raymond, PO Box 35, Exeter EX1 3YZ, UK, http://tinyurl.com/ctuulu6) is a growing collection of bibliographies to yet more newly published material in family history society journals and other sources, including the publications of the county and national record societies.

These bibliographies cover the whole British Isles, but for Scottish families you can also use M. Stuart's *Scottish Family History* (1930, repr. 1978) and P.S. Ferguson's *Scottish Family Histories* (1986). For Ireland, use B. de Breffny's *Bibliography of Irish Genealogy and Family History* (1964), E. MacLysaght's *Bibliography of Irish Family History* (1982), G.V. Flaming-Haigh's *Ireland: the Albert E. Casey Collection and other Irish materials in the Samford University Library: an Annotated Bibliography* (1976) and M.D. Falley's *Irish and Scotch-Irish Ancestral Research* (repr. 1998).

The catalogue of the British Library at http://catalogue.bl.uk/ is tremendously helpful. The Society of Genealogists has a substantial collection of privately printed family histories, all catalogued at www.sog.org.uk.

Many websites now reproduce pedigrees of aristocratic ancestors. Some are more reliable than others. Most are based, either accurately or loosely, on the earlier, printed pedigree material identified by

Visitation of Devon, edited by F. T. Colby, 110. *See* GEERE, GEARE.

GEREARDY. New England Register, lii. 313.

GERING. *See* GEARING.

GERLINGTON. Chetham Society, lxxxv. 119. *See* GIRLINGTON.

GERMAIN, or GERMAINE. Brydges' Collins' Peerage, vi. 306. Burke's Extinct Baronetcies.

GERMIN. Camden Society, xliii. 106. Visitation of Warwickshire, 1619, published with Warwickshire Antiquarian Magazine, 176. Harleian Society, xii. 169. *See* JERMIN.

GERNEGAN. The Genealogist, New Series, xvi. 39. *See* JERNINGHAM.

GERNET. *See* STOKEPORT.

GERNON. Morant's Essex, i. 13, 158 ; ii. 100, 179, 181, 232. Burke's Landed Gentry, 3, 4, 5, 6, 7, 8. History of the Parish of St. Leonard, Shoreditch, by Henry Ellis, 98. Proceedings of the Essex Archæological Society, v. 173. Wright's Essex, ii. 157. Memoirs of the family of Chester, by R. E. C. Waters, 187, 199. Banks' Baronies in Fee, ii. 85. Harleian Society, xli. 3. The Gresley's of Drakelow, by F. Madan, 257.

GERNONS. Weaver's Visitation of Herefordshire, 31.

GERNOUN. The Genealogist, New Series, ix. 212.

GERUNDE. Notes and Queries, 6 S. v. 5.

GERVIS, GERVAIS, GERVEIS, GERVEYS, GEIRVEIS, or GERVYS. Cambridgeshire Visitation, edited by Sir T. Phillipps, 15. Dwnn's Visitations of Wales, ii. 350. Burke's Commoners, ii. 340. Burke's Landed Gentry, 3, 4, 5, 7, 8. Harleian Society, ii. 71 ; ix. 75, 77 ; xli. 12, 32. Maclean's History of Trigg Minor, ii. 423, 427. Burke's Royal Descents and Pedigrees of Founders' Kin, 93. Nichols' History of the County of Leicester, ii. 671. An Historical Survey of Cornwall, by C. S. Gilbert, ii. 108. J. B. Payne's Armorial of Jersey, 162. The Visitations of Cornwall, edited by J. L. Vivian, 175. Miscellanea Genealogica et Heraldica, 3rd Series, ii. 59. The Genealogist, New Series, xvi. 231.

Printed sources for family histories catalogued in G.W. Marshall's The Genealogists' Guide.

these bibliographies, so to understand and verify online material it is sensible to go back and check the earlier printed sources. A site that seems reliable – it is based around the Burke's pedigrees – is www.thepeerage.com. Because it hyperlinks wives to their own family trees, the site helps you to explore up and down different lines and branches of families, discovering what interesting connections you can derive once you have traced your descent from an ancestor of aristocratic blood.

Just part of one of many, many shelves of printed family histories at the Society of Genealogists.

The Story Behind the Pedigrees

Before long, having plunged into this layered treasure trove of genealogical information, you will start finding discrepancies and omissions, so it is important to understand something of its own history. It is a story that sheds some light, too, on our own fascination with noble pedigrees, and reminds us that we share our interest with many people in the past – and that none of the information available to us now should be taken for granted.

Whilst interest in royal pedigrees goes back through the Middle Ages, and noble families were extremely proud of their ancestry, the majority of medieval records concerning noble families and their genealogies were resoundingly practical in their purposes.

The best examples are found in lawsuits over entitlement to land, privileges, titles or coats of arms. Many fine ones are in the Plea Rolls, which start in 1193. Many were extracted and published in Major General the Hon. G. Wrottesley's *Pedigrees from the Plea Rolls*, reprinted in the *Genealogist* (new series, v–xxi).

Such medieval pedigrees varied between two and seven or more generations. Most were based solely on the family's oral tradition, but some were compiled by clerks and monks, using monumental inscriptions, charters and other records in the family's own chest of muniments, and records of the local monasteries. Most noble families patronised monastic houses, and from the records of their gifts and endowments, and occasionally monastic chronicles which included the deaths of local aristocrats, valuable evidence could be gleaned. The 1378 Scrope v. Grosvenor case, in which the canons of Bridlington Priory used old charters to prove the ancestry of Sir Richard Scrope, is an early example of using old records as genealogical evidence.

In the 1400s came the first glimmerings of antiquarianism, a scholarly interest in the past based, not in mythology, but in a critical examination of surviving evidence. Early antiquarians who compiled collections of royal and noble pedigrees, drawing on both myth and original sources, included William Worcester alias Botoner (1415–82) and John Rous (fl. c. 1480).

This torch was then passed to the royal heralds. Their interest was in coats of arms, but as use of arms was hereditary, they were obliged to take an interest in the genealogy of the families concerned. Despite this, there is scant evidence of them taking genealogy very seriously until the late 1400s. The heralds were incorporated, as the College of Arms, by a royal charter of Richard III in 1484, and at this point they were given the tasks of discovering which families were using coats of arms by correct hereditary right, and punishing the many families who had simply adopted coats of arms of their own accord.

The result of their enquiries was the visitations, an early example of old records being used as genealogical evidence.

Chapter 9

THE VISITATIONS

Starting the Visitations

A visitation of Cheshire was made by William Ballard, March King of Arms, in about 1480 and one of the northern counties (probably by John Writhe, Norroy King of Arms, and his son Thomas Wriothesley, Garter King of Arms) in about the 1490s. A copy of the latter, edited by C.H. Hunter-Blair, is published in *Surtees Society*, Vol. 144.

The records varied from short pedigrees clearly taken down quickly from a familiy's personal, oral history, to long genealogies of the great northern houses, such as Percy, Neville and Fitzwilliam, in which family myths mixed freely with evidence taken from charters.

These were significant, but potentially isolated examples of English scholars taking an interest in genealogy. What came later – the sudden blossoming of England's love affair with genealogy – needed something pretty substantial to kick-start it.

Until the 1500s, medieval England and Wales looked back at history through the gilded prism of mythology. After the fall of Troy, they believed, Aeneas had fled from the burning city, and his settlement in Italy led to the foundation of Rome, as related in Virgil's *Aeneid*. In the AD 800s, the Welsh monk Nennius recorded a variety of pedigrees for a mythological British founding hero, Brutus, including one that made him Aeneas's great-grandson. By 1135, when Geoffrey of Monmouth wrote his monumental *History of the Kings of Britain*, Brutus had acquired a stirring story chronicling his journey from Rome to Britain, whose giants he killed and whose fertile land he settled with Trojan descendants. The same book recorded a version of what the Welsh bards had already been singing for several hundred years: a pedigree that came down from Brutus to the ancestors of the Welsh princes.

As a result of his victory at the Battle of Bosworth in 1485, Henry Tudor, a nobleman of royal English ancestry through his mother and grandmother, but of male-line Welsh ancestry through his father, became Henry VII of England. Galled by the impossibly long, mythically capped genealogies of the Scottish and French kings, Henry decided to trace his Welsh ancestry, so as to find his own descent from Brutus. A commission of Welsh genealogists, led by John Lleiaf and the bard Guttyn Owain, was told to find it.

Lleiaf and Owain were dismayed to discover that Henry's great-grandfather Meredith (Maredudd) ap ('son of') Tudor had been merely the butler to the Bishop of Bangor. But to keep their heads, they came to the wonderful conclusion that Meredith's father Tudor must in fact have been Tudor Fychan ap Gronow (d. 1367), whose wife Margaret was the sister of Owain Glendower's mother Ellen, and whose own ancestry linked back into Owain's own, purported descent from Brutus.

The wondrously long pedigrees sent back to London by the commissioners fascinated everyone. They appealed to the new royalty and nobility of the Tudor court, where even Henry VII himself had had to trace back four generations to find a king in his ancestry. Such long pedigrees conjured up the possibility of newly created aristocrats, sons of merchants and lawyers who had grown fat during the Wars of the Roses, being able to claim descent from anciently noble bloodlines, if only their genealogists could perform as miraculous a job for them as the Lleiaf-Owain commission had accomplished for the king.

It is in this context that we can better understand the sudden burgeoning of pedigree-recording, which took its most organised form in the Heralds' Visitations, one of the backbones of English genealogy. In 1498/9, Henry VII licensed the heralds to start making systematic county 'visitations', and they embarked on a vigorous series of periodic visitations of the English and Welsh shires. They were aided by hired deputies – local genealogists, such as Randle Holmes senior in Chester and no small number of Welsh genealogists in Wales. Their job was to police the use of coats of arms and, increasingly, to record the pedigrees of the armigerous families for their own sake. Admittedly, few families outside Wales had wondrously long pedigrees to record, but the growing fascination with recording descents over a number of generations *for their own sake* is apparent in the records.

The visitations continued, with particular bursts of activity in 1580, 1620 and 1666, until 1686. The Glorious Revolution of 1688 focused power in the hands of the great Whig lords, who were very little interested in the use of heraldry by the gentry, and the visitations ground to a halt. Abuse of heraldry resurged, but when the heralds asked the Deputy Earl Marshall to intervene in 1730, he refused: so many of his neighbours were misusing arms, he protested, that if he authorised a new visitation 'he should have all the County upon his back'.

Understanding the Visitations

The Heralds' Visitation pedigrees form the core of our knowledge of English genealogy. Titled families do not normally appear in visitations, because Garter King of Arms recorded them, individually, in the records of the College of Arms. The system was not flawless, so some families were simply left out by accident, whilst it is believed that some heralds deliberately excluded Catholics. But these are minor omissions: what is recorded is most of the social band below the nobility – the landed gentry and armigerous townsmen, merchants, clergy and other university educated professionals, and even some foreign, armigerous families settled in England, particularly in London.

No small number of visitation families were in fact younger branches of titled houses, whilst plenty of visitation families rose up, later, to attain titled status. From the younger branches of the visitation families descend innumerable families of labourers, many of whom migrated into the new cities of the Industrial Revolution.

As the visitations record the state of things before the disruption of industrialisation, they are a fair indication of who the landowners were, and how surnames were distributed, in medieval times. Many of the recorded lines go back into the 1400s, which is often only two or three centuries after surnames started becoming hereditary in the first place.

The pedigrees of the families using arms properly were written out initially in paragraphs: it was Robert Glover, Somerset Herald, who started using 'drop-line' pedigree charts in the 1570s, and the records are much the clearer as a result.

Some heralds like Sir Edward Bysshe (d. 1679) just recorded direct male lines, but others tried to record all the younger sons, and daughters, in living generations, and at least some of the recently dead generations too. It is rare to find a pedigree in which all children in each generation are recorded, and in assessing how complete a pedigree may be, it is important to look at the whole collection to see what level of detail was generally recorded, and how much was likely to have been left out.

If you have an unusual surname and find you come from the same area as a family recorded in the visitations, it is highly likely you will be related to them. Perhaps your line comes from a younger son not

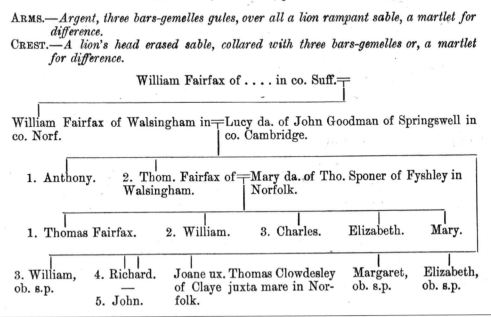

Fairfax.

Harl. 1552, ink fo. 51, pencil 47.

ARMS.—*Argent, three bars-gemelles gules, over all a lion rampant sable, a martlet for difference.*
CREST.—*A lion's head erased sable, collared with three bars-gemelles or, a martlet for difference.*

William Fairfax of . . . . in co. Suff.

William Fairfax of Walsingham in co. Norf. ═ Lucy da. of John Goodman of Springswell in co. Cambridge.

1. Anthony.   2. Thom. Fairfax of Walsingham. ═ Mary da. of Tho. Sponer of Fyshley in Norfolk.

1. Thomas Fairfax.   2. William.   3. Charles.   Elizabeth.   Mary.

3. William, ob. s.p.   4. Richard. —   5. John.   Joane ux. Thomas Clowdesley of Claye juxta mare in Norfolk.   Margaret, ob. s.p.   Elizabeth, ob. s.p.

The pedigree of Fairfax from 'The Visitations of Norfolk, 1563, 1589, and 1613', Harleian Society, Vol. 32 (1891). The reference 'Harl. 1552' relates to the source of the pedigree, in the Harleian Manuscripts in the British Library. There follows a blazon of the arms and crest the Fairfax family was using, and which the heralds duly authorised. As with many visitation pedigrees, the early generations, based on oral history, are not very detailed. Here, only the latter two are recorded in much detail, with sons numbered in order. 'ob. s.p.' is Latin: obit sine prole, 'died without children'; ux is Latin too, short for uxor, 'wife'.

shown in an early, sparsely recorded generation of the pedigree, or from a line that branched off before the top of the pedigree. Further research in original records may eventually show what that connection was.

The records were made at the time when many younger sons of gentry families were taking up land grants in New England. Even setting aside the tendency of nineteenth-century American genealogists to fantasise, the visitations really do include some founders of east-coast American families.

Initially, heralds visited churches and mansions, recording what they found, and what they were told. From 1566, those using arms were summoned to meet the heralds at the inns where they lodged.

Over roast meat and ale, the niceties of the pedigrees and use of arms was discussed and settled. Those using arms without authority were either quietly encouraged to pay for a new grant of arms, or they were ordered to stand in the market place and publicly 'disclaim' the coats of arms they had adopted without permission, and perhaps even see their flags and shields trampled in the mud.

Some visitation pedigrees stretch back into the Middle Ages. Faulty memory and sometimes snobbish fantasy – which was not always discouraged by heralds – means that the early sections of some pedigrees are unreliable. They can usually be checked and corrected using other records. But many are likely very accurate, and go back, using reliable family knowledge, beyond the scope of record-based research. As such they represent a unique and extraordinary resource for genealogists.

These images here and on the page opposite (the latter copied gingerly so as not to damage the spine of the book) show the evolution of the pedigree of my great-grandmothers' family the Havers of Thelveton, which appeared in Burke's Landed Gentry. *First came the Heralds' Visitation in 1664, and on this was based the pedigree in Blomefield's* History of Norfolk, *compiled in 1736 (see opposite). The Revd Blomefield added information provided by the family at the time. It was on this that the later Burke's pedigree was based.*

John Havers of Winfarthing.———Anne, daughter of - - - - Dussing of Brome.

Anne, married to Ed. Ward of Bixley	1. T. Havers of Winfarthing, died in 1605.	—Eliz. dr. of Wm. Dale.	2. William s. p. 4. Gawdy had issue.	3. Gilb. Receiver for Norf. 5. Edmund.

1. Wil. ob. s. p. 3 Edward 4. Tho. married Anne Ward, 1617. 5. Edmund. 6. Henry, married Elizabeth Ward. 7. Dale.

John Havers of Shelfhanger, heir in 1610.

Eliz. dr. of John Tindal of Banham.

Anne, married to T. Shardelow, Gent. Eliz. to W. Killingworth. Dorothy to John Whitefoot of Forncet. Frances, a nun. Judith to Wm. Brown. Mary to H. Tindall.

Clere Havers of Brakendale.

Wil. Havers, lord 1664.

Susan, dr. of - - - - - Brook of Whitchurch, Southam.

Richmond. s. p.

J. Havers of Norwich.

Mary, dr. of - - - - Collins of Southwold. Suffol.

Mary Englefield of Berkshire.

T. Havers, lord, ob. 1 Febr. 1697.

Alice, dr. and coheiress of Sir E. Moore of Kitlington, in Nottinghamsh. Bart. of Nova Scotia.

John. Susan married to T. Risden. Eliz. to H. Hudleston, Esq. of Sauston, in Cambridgsh. died in 1665.

Thom. Havers of Norwich, goldsmith.

Grace, dr. of Hen. Barney, of Anemere, Norfolk.

Wm. Havers, Esq. lord.———Mary Dormer.

Thomas, a religious. Henry. Mary, a nun at Bruges.

The College of Arms

The Heralds' Visitation books are at the College of Arms and are catalogued in Sir Anthony Wagner's *The Records and Collections of the College of Arms* (1952) and L. Campbell and F. Steer's *A Catalogue of Manuscripts in the College of Arms. Collections*, Vol. 1 (1988).

After the end of the visitations in 1686, the heralds continued to record pedigrees, both for people having new grants, and also anybody wanting to update visitation and other pedigree material already on record there. Meticulously cross-referenced, the College of Arms' records can bring lines right up to the present, and it is often worth paying the heralds' fees for a report on a family that is recorded there.

The College's collections also include the personal collections of many of its heralds, such as Ralph Bigland (1712–84), which has been catalogued by the Harleian Society in *The Bigland Pedigree Index* (1990). You can commission searches of the voluminous records of the College of Arms from the heralds, and they can yield stunningly good results. Its address is the College of Arms, Queen Victoria Street, London, EC4V 4BT, 0207 248 2762, www.college-of-arms.gov.uk.

Such records, however, were created ad hoc, and are not freely searchable. It fell, after 1686, to the antiquarian county historians to continue the work of researching and publishing the pedigrees of the nobility and gentry, and this they did with great enthusiasm.

The Harleian Society

When genealogists use visitation records, it is usually via the publications of the Harleian Society.

Almost as soon as the visitation records were made, copies were created, especially by heralds' deputies and herald painters. Some were accurate, and others were not. Some copies conflated several visitations made at different times, plus or minus the copyists' own knowledge, research and mistakes. These copies exist in manuscript collections, especially at Oxford and Cambridge colleges and the British Library ('BL', formerly British Museum, 'BM'). The latter in particular houses the Harleian Manuscripts ('Harl. Mss'), the genealogical and heraldic collection of Edward Harley, Earl of Oxford, which contains many copies of visitation pedigrees and the vast genealogical collections, themselves mainly visitation-based, of the four generations of Randle Holmses of Chester.

Some visitations have been published by record societies other than the Harleian Society, such as the Cheetham Society. In 1869, a group of genealogists founded the Harleian Society (Honorary Secretary, Harleian Society, College of Arms, Queen Victoria Street, London, EC4V 4BT, http://harleian.co.uk/), with the particular aim of publishing visitation pedigrees. Because the heralds wanted to keep their records to themselves, the society relied on the foregoing copies. W.H. Rylands, editor of the 'Visitations of Berkshire' (*Harleian Society*, Vol. 51 (1907)), wrote, for example, 'it has been my endeavour, *without having the use of the office copies*, to produce the various texts corresponding as nearly as possible to the original visitations taken by the Heralds'.

Using these copies, the Harleian Society has published a substantial number of the extant visitations. Its volumes can be examined in good libraries, especially those of the Society of Genealogists and the Institute of Heraldic and Genealogical Studies. The Harleian Society visitations are also now available on CD-ROM (www.archivecd books.ie/ and www.genealogysupplies.com/), and many are now free to view online, via the Medieval Genealogy website (http://tinyurl.com/2ary8m6).

The volumes are indexed, so besides looking at the pedigree for your surname, you can also check the pedigrees of other families into which they married, and from whom they took their wives. This way you will often be able to trace a whole network of connections amongst neighbouring families.

A complete index to all the pedigrees in all the visitations (and all who were 'disclaimed') is in C.R. Humphery-Smith's *Armigerous ancestors: a catalogue of sources for the study of the visitations of the heralds in the 16th and 17th centuries with referenced lists of names* (1997). This incorporates R. Sims's earlier *An Index to Pedigrees and Arms contained in the Heralds' Visitations and other Genealogical Manuscripts in the British Museum* (1849).

The Harleian Society has published several collections of pedigrees similar to the visitations, but made under different circumstances, such as Campling's *East Anglian Pedigrees* (pedigrees of families that generally are not in the visitations), Hunter's *Familiae Minorum Gentium* (mainly covering Yorkshire, Derbyshire, Cheshire and Lancashire), Le Neve's seventeenth-century *Pedigrees of Knights* and Charles Moor's *Knights of Edward I*.

William Berry's *County Genealogy* series (1830s), covering Berkshire, Buckinghamshire, Essex, Hampshire, Hertfordshire, Kent, Surrey and

Penruddocke of Compton Park, co. Wilts.

Arms.—Gules, a bend raguly argent.
Crest.—A demi-lizard's head rampant azure, armed and langued gules, between two eagle's wings expanded or.
Motto.—Soli Deo gloria.

Charles Penruddocke of Burcot, co. Somerset (2nd son of Charles Penruddocke of Compton Chamberlayne, M.P. co. Wilts, died 30 October 1788, by Anne Henrietta his wife, dau. of Wadham Wyndham of Fyfield, co. Wilts); of Wadham College, Oxford, matriculated 18 March 1796, aged 22; born 17 June 1773, and bapt. at Compton Chamberlayne the same day; died 6 November, bur. at Milston, co. Wilts, 11 November 1799, aged 25. Will dated 11 December 1799, proved 14 May 1800.

Martha, only dau. of John Band of Wookey House, co. Somerset; received into the Church at Wookey 22 October 1778; marr. at Wookey 30 September 1797 (marr. settlement dated 15 August 1793); died at 16 Great Ormond Street, London, 3 March, bur. at Milston, near Amesbury, co. Wilts, 11 March 1823, aged 43. Adm'on by her son Charles Penruddocke 24 May 1823.

Charles Penruddocke of Bath, Barrister-at-Law, born at Burcot 21 January, bapt. privately there 22 January and publicly at Milton, co. Wilts, 21 May 1799; died twelve o'clock Sunday night, 15 December, bur. at Bathwick Cemetery, Bath, 21 December 1839. Adm'on by his widow 20 February 1840. Tablet in St. Mary's Church, Bathwick.

Juliana Lætitia, eldest dau. of Capt. Thomas Penruddocke of Winkton, Ringwood, co. Hants, 3rd Foot Scots Fusilier Guards, by Juliana, dau. of George Lowther of Kilrue, co. Meath; born 15 August 1808, bapt. at Milton 15 June 1809; marr. at St. James's Church, Bath, by the Rev. Chambrè Brabazon Ponsonby Lowther, Rector of Orcheston St. George, co. Wilts, and maternal uncle to the bride, 15 February 1827; died 6 February, bur. at Milton Lilborne, Tuesday, 11 February 1890. Memorial Tablet in St. Mary's Church, Bathwick.

Charles Penruddocke of Compton Park, Fyfield, and Baverstocke, co. Wilts, and Bratton St. Maur, co. Somerset, educated at Eton, of Christ Church, Oxford, matriculated 20 October 1847, aged 19, of Inner Temple 1853, Barrister-at-Law, J.P. and D.L., High Sheriff 1861, Major Commandant 14th Wilts Rifle Volunteers, Captain Royal Wilts Yeomanry Cavalry, born at 1 Sion Place, Bathwick, Bath, on Tuesday, 30 September, at a quarter past five A.M., bapt. at St. Mary's, Bathwick, 1 October 1828.

Flora Henrietta, 2nd dau. of Walter Long, M.P., of Rood Ashton, co. Wilts, and Dolforgan, co. Montgomery; born 12 October, bapt. at Steeple Ashton, co. Wilts, 13 November 1827; marr. at St. George's, Hanover Square, London, 26 April 1853.

A page from Howard and Crisp's Visitation of England and Wales.

Sussex, comprises pedigrees based on the Heralds' Visitations for those shires, which he extended forwards through his own research.

The Visitation of England and Wales is a collection of visitation-style pedigrees (often including facsimile signatures) covering mainly eighteenth and nineteenth-century generations of families, compiled by two enthusiastic genealogists, Joseph Howard (1827–1902) and Frederick Crisp (1851–1922), published in twenty volumes from 1893.

There are numerous other works, in similar vein, for individual counties, of which J.J. Muskett's *Suffolk Manorial Families* (1900–11) is a fine example.

Wales, Ireland and Scotland

The Harleian Society has published a 'Catalogue of Welsh Manuscripts in the College of Arms'. Amongst the Welsh deputies employed by the English heralds was the bard Lewis Dwnn, who worked between 1586 and 1614: see the *Heraldic Visitations of Wales*, ed. Sir S.R. Meyrick (1846).

Ireland lacks visitation records, save for those held by Ulster King of Arms, which record non-Gaelic armigerous families settled in the 'Pale', in and around Dublin. The Chief Herald of Ireland (The Genealogical Office, 2–3 Kildare Street, Dublin 2, www.nli.ie) has the resulting records for Dublin (1568 and 1607) and Wexford (1618). The Chief Herald also has funeral certificates (1560–1690) recording the heraldry and family details of armigers whose funerals were marshalled by the Irish heralds.

In Scotland, where visitations were not held, the descent of armigerous families was recorded by Lord Lyon King of Arms (New Register House, Charlotte Square, Edinburgh, EH1 3YT, 0131 334 0380), both in birth briefs (or 'birthbrieves'), recording all sixteen great-grandparents of armigers, and lineal pedigrees. See F.J. Grant's *Index to genealogies, birthbriefs, and funeral escutcheons recorded in the Lyon office*, Scottish Record Society, old ser., 31, pt 40 (1908).

The County Histories

As the visitations continued, the heralds grew less credulous, and ever more keen to examine evidence and question critically what could really be proved.

Their development in critical thinking was paralleled by a growth in national scepticism. Henry VIII's Reformation had much to do with it:

if it was acceptable for the king to question the authority of the Pope, then everything else might be questioned too – including the accepted mythology concerning Britain's past.

It is ironic that Henry VIII, who laid as much stress upon his mythical British ancestry as his father had done, was the man who commissioned Polydore Vergil (*c.* 1470–1555), an Italian humanist and pioneer of critical thinking, to take a fresh look at British history. Perhaps Henry had hoped Polydore would confirm Britain's Trojan myth as correct, but the Italian's opinion, published as *Anglica Historia* in 1534, from the safety of the Continent, was withering. Brutus the Trojan, and his royal descendants, he said, were no more than a 'silly fiction'.

The arguments with which Polydore backed up his opinion were strong. Though it took a long time for his opinion to become widespread – there are still some who don't believe him – it had a highly disturbing effect on British psychology, for it swept away a vast swathe of detailed history that had previously been held as true, and replaced it with very little of any certainty at all. It was this void, caused by the sudden loss of Brutus, which antiquarians, as well as a host of proto-archaeologists, linguists, anthropologists, numismatists and scientists – none of whom had really existed before – sought desperately to fill. The alternative to such efforts – a profound ignorance of who we were and where we really originated – was simply too awful to contemplate.

One format favoured by antiquarians for their new explorations of our national past was the county history, which examined many aspects of a county's archaeology, history and prominent families. They start with William Lambarde's 1576 *Perambulation of Kent,* and early examples include Sampson Erdeswicke's *Survey of Staffordshire* (*c.* 1593–1603) and William Burton's *Description of Leicestershire* (1622). All such examples are teaming with pedigrees of landholding families.

Setting the tone for critical analysis of old records and monuments was the work of Sir William Dugdale (1605–86), Garter King of Arms, whose antiquarian works included *The Antiquities of Warwickshire, The Baronage of England* and *Monasticon Anglicanum* (a survey of the history and records of the dissolved monasteries). Though not so concerned with genealogies per se, the ongoing *Victoria County History* series produces volumes full of valuable details about the hereditary holders of manors, and through their efforts, the great work of county antiquarianism continues.

Sometimes, it is possible to see each stage in the creation of a grand, printed pedigree – how the family's visitation pedigree, combined with their own word of mouth knowledge of their recent origins, was improved by antiquarian research amongst funerary monuments and records, to become a pedigree in a county history – and how this then made its next transition, like that of a pupae into a butterfly – into the pages of Burke's.

Chapter 10

BURKE'S PEERAGE

Recording the Peerage

An innate, genealogical desire to sort pedigrees out, combined with a keen eye for profit, inspired several projects aimed at producing a complete set of pedigrees of the English nobility, building on the earlier, solid foundations laid by Dugdale. Besides being purchased by the families listed, these works were also scoured avidly by people seeking to prove their own aristocratic ancestry, perhaps to claim a title for themselves. They were also studied intently by parents on the make, seeking eligible, blue-blooded spouses for their own offspring.

It was Arthur Collins (1682–1760), a London bookseller, who first published such a work. His *Peerage of England* (1709) ran to three editions in his lifetime, and was followed by his equally important *Baronetage of England* (1720). The *Peerage of England* was based squarely on a copy of Dugdale's *Baronage*, which had been owned and updated by Gregory King, Lancaster Herald. Collins' *Peerage* was in turn updated later by Sir Egerton Brydges, and the successive editions show a transition from Collins's early, essay style, to a more regulated format that pre-empts the narrative style of Burke's.

Collins' *Baronetage of England* was a different enterprise altogether, for though he had a manuscript compiled by the great seventeenth-century genealogist Peter le Neve, he had in many cases to start from scratch because of the many baronetcies created since Le Neve's time. He often complained of the difficulty of coaxing baronets into sending him their pedigrees. This work was re-edited in 1741 by Thomas Wotton, so it is often known as 'Wotton's Baronetage'.

Both of Collins' works were full of good, solid genealogies, but unfortunately his constant need to flatter his patrons meant that he dared not prune back the occasional flights of fantasy he was sent, and in they went, however obviously fictitious they were. The St John family, for example, who arrived in England well after the Norman Conquest, wanted to believe their ancestor William had been 'grand master of the artillery' to William the Conqueror himself, and so that is what Collins repeated dutifully in his book.

Despite Collins's moans about the penury his work had brought him, his example was followed by Joseph Edmondson (d. 1786), whose *Baronagium Genealogicum* was based on a manuscript collection of 1708 by an earlier herald, Simon Segar.

THE

PEERAGE

O F

ENGLAND;

CONTAINING

A *Genealogical* and *Hiſtorical* ACCOUNT

Of all the

PEERS of *ENGLAND,*

Now exiſting, either by *Tenure*, *Summons* or *Creation :*
Their DESCENTS and COLLATERAL LINES:
Their BIRTHS, MARRIAGES, and ISSUES:
Famous ACTIONS both in *War* and *Peace:*
Religious and *Charitable* DONATIONS:
DEATHS, PLACES of *Burial*, MONUMENTS, EPITAPHS:
And many valuable Memoirs never before printed.

ALSO

Their Paternal COATS of *Arms*, CRESTS, *and* SUPPORTERS,
curiouſly engraven on COPPER PLATES.

Collected from *Records*, *Old Wills*, *Authentick Manuſcripts*,
our moſt approv'd *Hiſtorians*, and other Authorities.

By *ARTHUR COLLINS*, Eſq;

VOL. I.

The Second Edition, very much Enlarged, and Corrected.

LONDON:

Printed for W. INNYS at the *Weſt End* of St. *Paul's*, R. MANBY
on *Ludgate-Hill*, T. WOTTON and F. GOSLING in *Fleet-ſtreet*.
MDCCXLI.

Frontispiece to the 1741 edition of Collins' Peerage, in the Society of Genealogists.

FITZ-ROY Lord SOUTHAMPTON.

CHARLES, *the prefent Lord Southampton*, is brother to his Grace, Auguftus Henry, Duke of Grafton; under which title his Lordfhip's defcent may be feen in Vol. I. p. 189.

His Lordfhip was born June 25, 1737, and, on July 27, 1758, married Ann, daughter and co-heir of Sir Peter Warren, Knight of the Bath, and Vice Admiral of the Red fquadron, by whom he has iffue, now living;

George-Ferdinand, born Auguft 7, 1761, who is a Captain in the army, and one of the grooms of the bedchamber to the Prince of Wales.

Charles, born September 5, 1763.
Auguftus-William, born July 21, 1764.
Henry, born September 13, 1765.
Warren, born September 1, 1768.
Frederick, born October 10, 1769.
William, born December 12, 1773.
Robert, born May 27, 1775.
Edward-Somerfet, born October 25, 1776.
Ann-Caroline, born May 9, 1759.
Sufanna-Maria, born September 7, 1760.
Charlotte, born July 13, 1767.
Emily, born December 26, 1770.
Louifa, born December 12, 1771.
Georgaina, born October 13, 1782.
Alfo two fons and a daughter, which died infants.

An example of an entry from the 1784 edition of Collins's Peerage *(as edited by B. Longmate).*

Later works were built on these joint foundations, and on the genealogical work resulting from many eighteenth and early nineteenth-century lawsuits aimed at reviving old baronies by writ and other dormant or abeyant titles. Amongst these new works were George Kearsley's *Complete Peerage* (1794), Edmund Lodge's *The Genealogy of the Existing British Peerage* (1832), Joseph Foster's *The Peerage, Baronetage and Knightage of the British Empire for 1880* (1881–2) and James E. Doyle's *Official Baronage of England* (1886).

The most important, however, are the publications of Debrett and Burke, and the *Complete Peerage* and *Complete Baronetage*, both compiled by the George Edward Cokayne (1825–1911), Clarenceaux King of Arms, known as 'G.E.C.'. G.E.C.'s books catalogued the successive holders of titles in considerable academic detail. In Scotland, James Balfour Paul edited the impressive *The Scots Peerage*, 8 vols (1904–14), based on J.P. Wood's earlier edition of Sir Robert Douglas's 1764 *Peerage of Scotland.*

Aside from these printed sources, and as a point of cross-reference, if necessary, there are manuscript pedigrees of all peers admitted to the House of Lords from 1767 to 1802 in the Parliamentary Archives.

In 1802, John Debrett produced the first edition of his *Peerage*, followed by his *Baronetage* in 1808: the two were later united in a single volume, new editions of which then continued to appear regularly. They focused on the living rather than on ancestors, so, like G.E.C., they have a limited use for those of us who are most interested in tracing links back to the aristocracy via daughters and younger sons.

ORANMORE AND BROWNE, BARON. (Browne-Guthrie.)

GEOFFREY DOMINICK AUGUSTUS FREDERICK BROWNE-GUTHRIE, 2nd Baron, and a Representative Peer; *b.* 1819; *s.* 1860; ed. at Harrow, and at Trin. Coll., Camb.; is a J.P. and D.L. for cos. Ayr and Mayo (High Sheriff 1841); assumed additional name of Guthrie on his marriage: *m.* 1859, Christina, who *d.* 1887, only child and heiress of the late Alexander Guthrie, Esq., of the Mount, Ayrshire, and has issue.

Arms,—Barry of eight or and azure, an eagle displayed with two heads sable, surrounded by an orle of martlets gules. Crest,—A griffin's head erased.

Boldly and faithfully.

Supporters—Dexter, a knight in chain armour, proper, holding in the exterior hand a battle-axe, and on the sinister arm a shield argent, charged with two lions passant guardant; *sinister*, a like knight, the armour covered by a surtout argent, and hanging from the sinister arm a shield argent, thereon the arms of Browne.

Seats,—Castle-Macgarrett, Claremorris, co. Mayo. , *Clubs,*—Carlton, Kildare Street, National.

SON LIVING.

Hon. GEOFFREY HENRY BROWNE, *b.* Jan. 6th, 1861; ed. at Trin. Coll., Camb. (B.A. 1882, M.A. 1886); formerly Lieut. 4th Batn. Royal Scots Fusiliers; is a J.P. for Ayrshire, and a J.P. and a D.L. for co. Mayo (High Sheriff 1890). *Clubs,*—White's, Bachelors'.

DAUGHTER LIVING.

Hon. Mary Christina Browne, *b.* 1862: *m.* 1890, Maurice des Graz, Esq. *Residences,*—The Firs, Wimbledon; 33, Tedworth Square, S.W.

PREDECESSOR.—[1] DOMINICK Browne, *P.C.*, M.P. for and Lord Lieut. of co. Mayo, was cr. *Baron Oranmore and Browne* (peerage of Ireland) 1836; *b.* 1787: *m.* 1811, Catherine Anne, el. dau. and co.-heir of Henry Monck, Esq.; *d.* 1860; *s.* by his son [2] GEOFFREY DOMINICK AUGUSTUS FREDERICK, 2nd Baron and present peer.

A typical entry from Debrett's.

He *d.* unm., 3 Feb. 1642/3, aged 27.

III. 1643.   3. ALEXANDER (ERSKINE), EARL OF KELLIE, &c. [S.], br. and h., was served h. to his brother 18 Apr. 1643 ; was a zealous Royalist ; Col. of Foot for the counties of Fife and Kinross, was in the " engagement " of 1648 to attempt the rescue of the King ; was sent by the Parl. [S.], 12 June 1649, to Charles II in Holland, for whom he fought at Worcester, 1651, where he was taken prisoner.   He was excepted from Cromwell's Act of Grace, 1654.   P.C. [S.] 1 Oct. 1661.   He *m.*, 1stly, in 1661, Anna, da. of Col. John KIRKPATRICK, Gov. of Bois-le-Duc.   He *m.*, 2ndly (cont. 8 July 1665), Mary, da. of Sir John DALZELL, of Glenae, co. Dumfries, by Agnes, da. of James NISBET, of Restalrig.   She was living in 1677.   He *d.* May 1677.

IV. 1677.   4. ALEXANDER (ERSKINE), EARL OF KELLIE, &c. [S.],

An entry from G.E.C.'s Complete Peerage.

Burke's Peerage

Of much greater use were the works initiated by John Burke (1786–1848), an Irish-born printer and genealogist who settled in London and produced his first *Peerage and Baronetage* in 1826. It was based heavily on all that had gone before, particularly the work of Collins.

The **6th Marquess** *m* 2nd 23 April 1960 (*divorce* 1972) Lady (Anne) Juliet Dorothea Maud Wentworth Fitzwilliam, MA Oxford (*m* 2nd, as his 4th w, Somerset de Chair), only child of 8th Earl Fitzwilliam, DSC (*see* 1970 edn), and by her had:

2a (Frederick William Charles) Nicholas Wentworth; *b* 26 Nov 1961; *educ* Eton and Yale; *d* by his own hand 26 Jan 1998

1a Ann; *b* and *d* 24 Feb 1966

The **6th Marquess** *m* 3rd 12 July 1974 •Yvonne Marie, only dau of Anthony Sutton, of Woodstook, The Glen, Farnborough Park, Kent, and *d* 1985, having by her had:

3a FREDERICK WILLIAM AUGUSTUS HERVEY, **8th and present Marquess of Bristol**

2a •Victoria Frederica Isabella; *b* 6 Oct 1976; model

3a •Isabella Frederica Louisa; *b* 9 March 1982; model first with Models Frontiers agency then Premier Model Management

Part of the Marquess of Bristol's entry in Burke's Peerage, *showing the narrative style of all the Burke's publications.*

Burke's Peerage appeared in regular updates produced by Burke, his son and successor, Sir (John) Bernard Burke (1814–92), Ulster King of Arms, and several grandchildren throughout the nineteenth century. New editions were published regularly during the nineteenth and twentieth centuries, adding notices of knights (but not knights' pedigrees). The last paper edition (the 107th), edited by Charles Mosley, appeared in 2003, and soon after it appeared online at www.burkespeerage.com/. Mosley's edition included for the first time the pedigrees of Scottish clan chiefs: up to then, many clan chiefs who happened also to hold titles of nobility were included, but the 107th edition included them all, titled or not.

Burke's success led to the production of *A Genealogical and Heraldic History of the Commoners of Great Britain and Ireland*, 4 vols (1833–7), reprinted in a fully indexed version 1842–8 and then updated (but not indexed) as *Burke's Landed Gentry of Great Britain and Ireland*, which has appeared in many subsequent editions up to 2001. The latest version is also searchable on www.burkes-peerage.net. Over the years, the Burke's publishing house in its various incarnations has produced many other useful genealogical works as well, including *A Genealogical and Heraldic History of the Colonial Gentry*, *Irish Families* and *Royal Families*, and it is interesting to dip into *Vicissitudes of Families* too.

Burke's has also covered titles that have become dormant or extinct – partly because their genealogies are still relevant to people who are descended (through daughters) from those families, and also because of the great fascination with the prospect of reviving old titles. The books are Sir B. Burke's *A Genealogical History of the Dormant, Forfeited and Extinct Peerages of the British Empire* (1831, rev. edn 1883) and *Burke's A Genealogical and Heraldic History of the Extinct and Dormant Baronetcies of England, Ireland and Scotland* (1841). Also useful in this context – though not Burke's publications themselves – are *The Dormant and Extinct Baronage of England* (1807), containing wonderful folded pedigree charts, and L.G. Pine's *The New Extinct Peerage 1884–1971* (1972).

Unlike most of the earlier works that came before, and were concerned primarily with the successive heads of important families, the Burke's publications focused on genealogy. The pedigrees went back not just to the first holder of a title, but as far back as they could, to the earliest traceable ancestor or founder of the family. Burke put in full dates of birth, marriage and death (Debrett usually just stated years). Besides the succession of elder sons, Burke sought to chronicle

Part of the Society of Genealogists' fine collection of volumes of Burke's Peerage.

younger sons and, from the mid-nineteenth century onwards, those sons' descendants too, providing fuller and more inclusive accounts of the families concerned – and of course increasing the number of people mentioned, who would be likely to want to buy the book.

Daughters were never so well chronicled, sometimes being lumped together simply as 'other issue', but if you examine the same pedigree in a number of different editions of Burke's, you will sometimes find them being included, then being pruned out to save space, perhaps only to reappear again in later volumes.

Remember that families whose titles became extinct or who lost their land will vanish from later editions of Burke's, and newly risen or ennobled families will appear. By working through successive volumes, you will be able to watch the story of a family, and its view of itself, developing and changing as the decades roll past.

Burke's Family Index, published by Burke's in 1976, indexes the huge number of pedigrees in all the Burke's publications. The bibliographies of Whitmore, Marshall and so on, referred to earlier, also cover Burke's very well.

Burke's Style

Burke's developed a distinctive 'narrative' style so as to include a vast amount of genealogical information in as few pages as possible. The style takes us right back to the roots of recorded genealogy, to Hesiod, who chronicled the pedigree of the gods in poetry, but his prototype style was improved here by use of indented paragraphs and numbering. The system will likely confuse you at first, as it takes some time and practice to master. When reading a Burke's pedigree, I usually sketch out a simple family tree on paper, to make it easier to follow.

Burke starts with the earliest ancestor. For the first few generations, there will probably just be a list of successive heads of the family. As we come forward in time, there will usually be more detail on the heads, and who they married. When wives came from families who are also in Burke's, this is indicated by *q.v.* (*quod vide*, 'which see'). Then, the children are listed, first all the boys, and then all the girls:

Cuthbert, for example, had the following issue:

1. John, his heir
2. Thomas
3. William

Then, John has his own paragraph, and his children are listed below him, and so on. The pedigrees become complicated when Burke's follows down the lines of younger sons. This is done by further indentations:

Cuthbert had the following issue:

1. John, his heir
2. Thomas married and had children, who are indented further:
   1. Fred
   2. Harry
   3. George. If George then has his own children, they are indented even more:
      1. Edward
      2. Eustace
   4. Charles
3. William

Thus, Edward and Eustace are children of George, grandchildren of Thomas and great-grandchildren of Cuthbert.

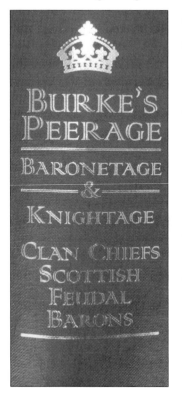

Different editions of Burke's use numbers slightly differently: some have no numbering at all, others are as shown above, and the more recent editions also give a letter to each indented generation – so the eldest son of 2a is numbered 2b – which is supposed to make matters clearer. It is the indentations themselves that are the key to success here: by running your finger back up the page you can follow the generations back to the source.

Once you are used to it, you will find this system so useful and flexible that you may want to use it yourself, to record families of any social background. It is my preferred method of recording genealogical information, and it works very well in normal Word documents on normal computers. The beauty of mastering the system is that you will not need to buy

The cover of the 107th edition of Burke's Peerage.

some of the plethora of computer programmes that have been devised to store genealogical information, but whose complex and repetitive nature makes them very restricting and confusing. This system contains no repetition at all, save the names of the next heirs in turn.

Reforming Burke's

Towards the end of the nineteenth century, the genealogical world was shaken by John Horace Round (1854–1928). He was an icono-clastic scholar who sought out, attacked and demolished any pedigrees, particularly those in Burke's, that contained inaccuracies, or myths – and all with a memorable degree of savagely intellectual venom. Single-handedly, Round's scholarly pen cleared the battlefield of Hastings of half its alleged Norman participants. So researching a family in Burke's should not rely on one volume alone: the early ones give family myths, whilst the later editions will often contain quite different and much more scholarly views of the true origins. See W. Page (ed.), *Family Origins and other studies, by the late J. Horace Round M.A., LL D* (1930).

Round improved Burke's a lot, but even its latest editions are not perfect. Especially for generations before the start of the nineteenth century, your research may turn up other sons, or any daughters at all born to the family, contradict published dates and highlight all manner of errors and omissions. However, if you are going to claim your research is superior to the material in Burke's, make jolly sure you have undertaken your work accurately and objectively, and that you can back up your views with cast-iron evidence.

To make a connection with a Burke's (or other printed) pedigree, you will usually need to do some original research both on the generations leading back to it, and also on the connecting generation in Burke's itself. For example, your ancestor was baptised in 1780, and you think his father was a younger son in a Burke's pedigree. It will help to prove that that the younger son married soon before 1780, and died sometime after 1780. His will may name and confirm that he had a son, who was the same person as your ancestor. His own father, or close relatives, might also mention your direct ancestors. You may find that your family lived on land that had previously been owned by the main stem of the 'Burke's' family. All this requires original research in original records, the subject of our next chapter.

Horace Round, the great reformer of the semi-fictional pedigrees in the early volumes of Burke's.

The Route to the Jermyns

One of the family connections I discovered during my research, which is of most significance to me, is that I am an ancestral great-nephew of Henry Jermyn, Earl of St Albans. But how do I know this? The printed pedigree of my Havers ancestors in *Burke's Commoners* (which became *Burke's Landed Gentry*) shows that my ancestor Thomas

Havers married Henrietta (or Harriott) Maria D'Ewes, daughter of Sir Symonds D'Ewes of Stowlangtoft, 'bart', i.e., baronet. His family is not in *Burke's Peerage*, which includes all baronetcies that are still extant, so instead I looked in *Burke's Extinct Baronetcies*. Illustrated here is a section of their pedigree, showing 'Harriott' and her sisters, and identifying her mother as Delariviere, daughter of Thomas, Lord Jermyn. That peerage is extinct, so the Jermyn pedigree is in *Burke's Extinct Peerage*: the short section of that reproduced here picks the trail up and shows the link to the Jermyns.

Sir Willoughby died 13th June, 1685, and was *s.* by his son,

III. SIR SYMONDS D'EWES, who *m.* Delariviere, daughter and co-heir of Thomas, Lord Jermyn, and by her, who died in 1702, had issue,

    I. JERMYN, his heir.
    II. Willoughby, *d.* in 1710, aged nineteen.
    III. Symonds, *d.* 1693.
    IV. Thomas, *d.* 1698.

    I. Delariviere, *m.* to Thomas Gage, esq. eldest son of Sir Thomas Gage, bart.
    II. Mary, *m.* to George Tasburgh, esq. of Bodney, in Norfolk, by whom she had one son,

        George Tasburgh, who *m.* first, in 1755, Teresa, daughter of Thomas, Viscount Gage, which lady died *s. p.* in 1773, and secondly, Barbara, daughter of Thomas Fitzherbert, esq. of Swinnerton, by whom he had no issue. Mr. Tasburgh's widow wedded, for her second husband, George Crathorne, esq. of Crathorne, and died in 1808, leaving a daughter, Mary-Anne-Rosalia Crathorne.

    III. Harriott, *m.* to Thomas Havers, esq. of Thelton Hall, Norfolk, and from this marriage descends the present

        THOMAS HAVERS, esq. of Thelton Hall. (See BURKE's *Commoners*, vol. i. p. 381.)

    IV. Merelina, *m.* to Richard Elwes, esq.

Sir Symonds died in May, 1722, and was *s.* by his son,

    IV. SIR JERMYN D'EWES, who died unm. 21st April, 1731, when the BARONETCY became EXTINCT.

The 2nd son,

HENRY JERMYN, master of the horse to the queen, having devoted himself with a more than ordinary degree of zeal to the fortunes of his royal master, during the civil wars, was elevated to the peerage, 8 September, 1643, as BARON JERMYN, *of St. Edmundsbury, co. Suffolk*, with remainder, in default of male issue, to his elder brother, Thomas Jermyn. His lordship subsequently attended the queen into France, and presided over her majesty's small establishment for a great many years. While abroad he was employed in several embassies by King CHARLES II., and in consideration of all his faithful services, his lordship, immediately upon the Restoration, was created, by letters patent, dated at Breda, 27 April, 1660, EARL OF ST. ALBANS. He was soon after made a knight of the Garter, and constituted lord chamberlain of the household. His lordship *d. unm.* in 1683, when the Earldom of St. Albans became EXTINCT, and the Barony of Jermyn devolved upon (his deceased brother Thomas's son,) his nephew,

THOMAS JERMYN, 2nd Baron Jermyn. This nobleman was governor of Jersey. By Mary, his wife, he had issue,

A dau. ——, *m.* to Thomas Bond, Esq., and *d.* in the life-time of her father.

Mary, *m.* to Sir Robert Davers, Bart.

Merelina, *m.* 1st, to Sir William Spring, and 2ndly, to Sir William Gage, Bart., of Hengrave, but had no issue.

Penelope, *m.* to Grey-James Grove, Esq.

Delarivierre, *m.* to Sir Symonds D'Ewes, Bart.

He *d.* in 1703, when the Barony of Jermyn, of St. Edmundsbury, became EXTINCT.

The information in this pedigree of Jermyn from Burke's Extinct Peerage *dovetails with that of D'Ewes on the previous page.*

Chapter 11

ORIGINAL SOURCES

General Sources

Printed sources aside, tracing back to find and prove aristocratic ancestors, and researching the origins of aristocrats themselves, is not very different to tracing any other sort of ancestor. This chapter is not intended as a comprehensive guide to all the records you could possibly use for this, but rather as a summary of those sources that are particularly useful for tracing back to aristocratic forebears, and for learning more about families with blue blood.

Working back in time, **General Registration Office** (GRO) birth, marriage and death certificates began to be issued in 1837 (1855 in Scotland and 1864 in Ireland, with Protestant marriages there back to 1845). These can be used in tandem with census returns from 1911 back to 1841, except in Ireland, where few survive before 1901.

England and Wales's GRO and census material is indexed on sites including www.genesreunited.com, www.findmypast.com and www.thegenealogist.co.uk. Ireland's 1901 and 1911 censuses are at www.census.nationalarchives.ie/, and General Registration is with the two registrars general, in Belfast and Dublin. Many Scottish resources, including General Registration, censuses, Old Parochial Registers (as they termed parish registers), and wills and testaments (and coats of arms) are on www. scotlandspeople.gov.uk.

Going back further are **parish registers**, which one of my own aristocratic ancestors, Thomas Cromwell, Earl of Essex, introduced in 1538. Most actually survive from the late 1500s/early 1600s onwards. You can use the baptisms, marriages and burials they record to piece together lines of ancestry, and add detail to sources such as the visitations.

Some sources for the very poor are useful too. When a family moved into a parish, they handed in a **settlement certificate**, issued by their parish of origin, identifying that parish as liable to pay for their upkeep, should they fall into poverty. These can be used to chart the movements of labouring families back, parish by parish, to where, in some fortunate cases, their ancestor had been the younger son of a gentry family, identified in a Heralds' Visitation pedigree. Those that survive exist in the **parish chest** collection for the relevant parish, now mostly archived in county record offices.

The details of how to use such sources, and many more, are in Simon Fowler's *Tracing Your Ancestors* (2011) and my own *Tracing Your Family History* (2004/2008), *Tracing Your Irish Family History* (2007) and *Tracing Your Scottish Family History* (2008).

For all material in this chapter identified as being at The National Archives, see the relevant research guide at http://tinyurl.com/cz6dnre.

Birth, Marriage and Death

Plenty of well-to-do families' births, marriages and deaths were announced in **newspapers** and periodicals, particularly the *Gentleman's Magazine* (1871–1922), for which there are a number of published indexes (all at the Society of Genealogists).

British newspapers are kept in the British Library's newspaper library (in north London, but about to be transferred to Yorkshire), http://tinyurl.com/mbf6yj and are increasingly being indexed online: www.genesreunited.com has a growing collection, as has http://www. britishnewspaperarchive.co.uk. You can also explore the Burney Collection of seventeenth- and eighteenth-century newspapers at http://tinyurl.com/9w2ngqt (it can be accessed free at The National Archives and in some university libraries), and also the *Illustrated London News* at www.iln.org.uk/ and The *Times* is at http://archive. timesonline.co.uk/tol/archive.

The real fathers of illegitimate children were sometimes recorded in **bastardy bonds**, found in parish-chest material in county archives. Few aristocrats were humiliated in this way, though, and these records are more likely to quash a story that your illegitimate ancestor was the son of a duke, than prove it.

Details of legitimate heirs were recorded in **Inquisitions Post Mortems** (IPMs). Held by the royal Escheators on the death of a tenant-in-chief (one who held land direct from the Crown) from 1235 to 1662, the inquisitions recorded the name and age of the deceased's heir. The records are in The National Archives (C 133-142 and E 149-150). Many have been published by county record societies. Many published volumes of abstracts are at www.british-history.ac.uk. You will often find 'IPM' as a reference in an aristocratic pedigree, as they are so useful in reconstructing family lines.

When the heir was a boy underage (21) or a girl under 14, they would become a **ward of Chancery**. The Crown appointed a guardian (usually the appointment was a favour granted to a loyal follower). The guardian took the profits of the estate (allowing from this a grant or 'exhibition' for the heir's maintenance and education), until the heir came of age or the heiress married: an heiress's hand in marriage was a lucrative gift that the Crown could bestow on a loyal follower, whether the girl wanted it or not. The Chancery records are in The National Archives (class C) and the best finding aid is The National Archives' online catalogue. The system was further institutionalised under the **Court of Wards and Liveries**, which existed from 1541 to 1660. Records are in The National Archives (class WARD 1-15).

Upper class families often made **marriage settlements**, which were deeds signed before weddings, arranging for the future owner-ship of property. Parents might settle property or income on one of the two parties marrying, often as a **dowry**, which was the land or money brought into the marriage by the bride. Grooms or their families would guarantee a **dower**, which was property or income for the use of their bride in widow-hood, but which reverted to the family's estate after her death. Marriage settlements are often found in family papers (in private hands or archives). There are many in the manuscripts section of the British Library, and a good num-ber were collected and abstracted by Frederick Crisp in *Fragmenta Genealogica*, Vol. 11. They are

An aristocratic obituary from the Coventry Standard, *4 August 1961.*

LADY BELINDA DUGDALE DIES AT AGE OF 36

THE death took place in Queen Elizabeth Hospital in Birmingham on Saturday of Lady Belinda Dugdale, wife of Captain W. S. Dugdale, of Blyth Hall, Coleshill, and second daughter of the Earl of Radnor.

Lady Belinda, who was 36, was married in December, 1952 and had four children, three girls and a boy. The eldest girl is aged seven and the others, twins, are six. The son was born in February, 1959, and is in direct line for the Dugdale baronetcy.

His birth caused great jubilation and was celebrated later that year at a cocktail party attended by tenants and estate employees at Merevale Hall, near Atherstone, the home of Capt. Dugdale's parents, Sir William Francis Stratford Dugdale and Lady Dugdale.

LOVED AND ADMIRED

Loved and admired by coun-try people, villagers and estate workers alike, Lady Belinda was noted for her kindness and the

---

Thomas, Marquis of Dorset.

Inquisition taken at the Guildhall, 30 November, 24 Henry VIII [1532], before *Stephen Peycoke*, Mayor and escheator, after the death of *Thomas*, late *Marquis of Dorset*, by the oath of *William Davys, John Briggs, Thomas Robynson, John Twyford, William Mosseman, Andrew Chesham, William Roydon, Nicholas Nolthorp, Richard Harrys, John Hawthorn, Roger Taylor, Stephen Benett, Richard Madock, William Wycherley*, and *Ralph Harbotell*, who say that

Thomas, late **Marquis** of *Dorset*, after he married the *Lady Margaret*, late his wife (who still survives), was seised of the large messuage or tenement in the parish of St. James at Garlyke Hythe within the ward of Vintrey, and of 9 messuages situate in the parish of St. Andrew in the ward of Barnardez Castell.

All the said premises are held of the King in free burgage: the messuage in the parish of St. James is worth per ann., clear, 40s., and the said 9 messuages are worth per ann., clear, 46s. 8d.

The said Marquis died 10 October, 22 Henry VIII [1530]: *Henry Gray*, now Marquis of *Dorset*, is his son and next heir, and was then aged 13¾ years, 12 weeks, 4 days and more.

Inq. p. m. 24 Henry VIII, No. 97.

A printed copy of the London Inquisition Post Mortem for Thomas, Marquess of Dorset, from G.S. Fry's Abstracts of Inquisitions Post Mortem for the City of London, *Part 1, available at www.british-history.ac.uk.*

sometimes referred to and abstracted in family wills ('whereas by a deed of settlement dated . . .'). They provide excellent details not only of who was getting married and when, but also names of relatives on both sides, family friends who acted as guarantors and witnesses and the location and nature of lands held.

Instead of having banns called in the parish church, most aristocratic couples (and many others with social pretensions) chose to

---

Manby 1729   Abbott 252

THOMAS MANBY of SOUTHWEALD, Co. ESSEX, Knight

Will dated 23rd April, 1729. Not more than £40 for funeral. Whereas by
Deed of Marriage Settlement dated 5th September, 1694 between Sir Thos. Manby
of Lincolns Inn, Middx, Knight, 1st part, Elizabeth Cary daughter of Sir
George Cary of Torr Abbey, Devon, 2nd part and Sir Francis Wyndham of Trent,
Co. Somerset, Bt. Sir Robert Throgmorton of Weston, Bucks. and Charles Cranmer
of St. Clement Danes, Middx, Esq., 3rd part £2,000 is settled by said Sir Thos.
Manby on these trees for use of his children by said E. Cary on trust for said
Sir. Thos. and his lady for lives and then for such children as parents appoint
and in default equally. I appoint as follows, my son Robert to have said land

---

Marriage settlements are sometimes quoted in wills. This is a typescript genealogical abstract (a summary of all the relevant information, minus all the legal jargon) of a will that opens with a recitation of one.

marry by licence. **Marriage licences** ('M. Lics.') can survive from as far back as the 1300s. Apart from some issued by the Archbishop of Canterbury, which allowed the marriage to take place anywhere, marriage licences usually specify one of two places where the marriage could take place, normally the bride's and groom's home parishes. They were issued by the same local church authorities – generally archbishops, bishops and archdeacons – that proved wills. Their whereabouts is detailed in J. Gibson's *Bishops' transcripts and marriage licences, bonds and allegations* (4th edn, 1997).

Until it became widely available in 1943, the complexity and expense of **divorce** excluded most ordinary families, making it the preserve of the wealthy and aristocratic. Up to 1858, divorce was possible only by a private Act of Parliament, records of which are held in the Parliamentary Archives (Private Bill Office, original acts HL/PO/PB/1, from 1547). For 1858 to 1943, divorces are in The National Archives class J 77, searchable at www.catalogue.national archives.gov.uk, although few for 1937–43 survive. Those after 1943 are held at the Principal Registry of the Family Division (First Avenue House, 42–9 High Holborn, London, WC1V 6NP). Scottish divorce records are at the Scottish Record Office.

Paupers often went to their graves with no more than a brief entry in a burial register, but the higher up the social scale you go, the more records exist which were generated by death.

Most well-to-do people, including aristocratic ancestors and their immediate descendants, left **wills**. In England, Wales and Ireland, most wills were proved in Church courts up to 1858 and then in civil ones thereafter, collected at the Principal Probate Registries for England and Wales (First Avenue House, 42–9 High Holborn, London, WC1V 6NP): those for Ireland are in The National Archives in Dublin and the Public Record Office of Northern Ireland (though few before 1922 survive).

Before 1858, whilst wills could be proved by various Church courts, most aristocratic ones are in the Prerogative Courts of Canterbury and York (and Dublin, for Ireland). If a will had not been written, letters of administration might be taken out and recorded in the same places. An administrator was often the next of kin. A will can name spouses and children, grandchildren, siblings, nephews and nieces and many more besides, and may mention the inheritance of lands, artefacts and family portraits. In the best scenarios, a run of detailed wills can prove a pedigree almost single-handed.

Scottish wills and testaments (1513–1901) are indexed on www. scotlandspeople.gov.uk and most later ones are at The National Archives of Scotland.

For the period 1796 to 1903, many English and Welsh wills were abstracted in Estate Duty (also called Death Duty) registers, at The National Archives in class IR 26, indexed in IR 27, fully indexed on www.findmypast.com. It is interesting to see who actually received what from a will: granny may have been bequeathed a million pounds in her father's will, but if he died nearby bankrupt, she may only have received ten shillings and sixpence!

Grave stones or, for the very grand, monuments in churches, together termed '**monumental inscriptions**' (MIs), provide useful genealogical details and may include family heraldry – a good clue about aristocratic origins. The website www.deceasedonline.co.uk/ has a growing database of municipal burial and cremation records. Many MIs have been transcribed and these can be found in local archives or in print, particularly the *English Church Brasses* series and *Transactions of the Monumental Brass Society*, and Ireland's the 'Memorials of the Dead', *Journal of the Association for the Preservation of the Memorials of the Dead* (1888–1937).

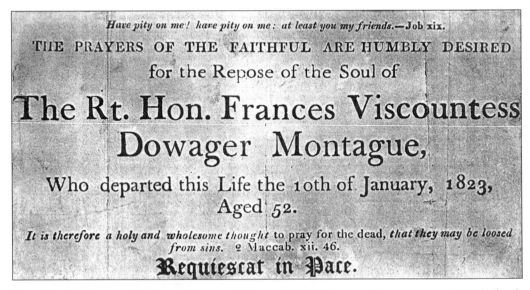

From about 1800 onwards, it becomes increasingly common to find memorial or prayer cards in the family papers of well-to-do Catholics. This is an early example, bigger than most later ones, from my family papers. Their main genealogical use is supplying a date of death and an age.

Sir Reginald de Braybroke (d. 1405), being prayed for by his sons Reginald and Robert on a brass at Cobham, Kent (from English Church Brasses*).*

At Ledbury, Herefordshire, the wife of the Rev. W. H. Lambert, a son.

At Westbourne-place, the wife of Capt. W. R. Lascelles, Rifle Brigade, a dau.

At Cardiston, Salop, the wife of the Rev. H. D. Lloyd, a son.

At Stuston, Scole, Norfolk, the Hon. Mrs. Edwd. Paget, a son.

At Oxford, the wife of C. A. Chetwynd Talbot, esq., of Aston, Cheshire, a dau.

Dec. 22. At Cattistock Lodge, Dorchester, the Lady Poltimore, a son.

At Colchester, the wife of the Rev. J. G. Bingley, M.A., a son.

The wife of Charles Combe, esq., of Cobham-park, Surrey, a son.

At Howbury Hall, Bedfordshire, the wife of F. C. Polhill-Turner, esq., a dau.

At Bradford-on-Avon, the wife of the Rev. J. C. Thring, a dau.

Dec. 23. At Princes-gate, Lady Louisa Fielding, a son.

Dec. 26. At Cockfield Hall, Suffolk, Lady Blois, a son.

At Southfield, Stirling, the wife of Sir A. G. Hay, bart., of Park, a dau.

In Belgrave-road, the wife of Comm. H. McClintock Alexander, R.N., a dau.

At Mount Royd, Bradford, the wife of W. H. Peel, esq , a dau.

At Limerick, the wife of Lieut.-Col. Vesey, R.A., a son.

Dec. 27. At Edinburgh, the Hon. Mrs. Lake Gloag, a dau.

At Norwich, the wife of the Rev. J. Dombrain, of St. Benedict, a dau.

At Rhydoldy, Rhayader, the wife of R. L. Lloyd, esq , barrister-at-law, a dau.

At West Derby, Liverpool, the wife of T. Makins, esq., barrister-at-law, a son.

At St. Leonard's-on-Sea, the wife of the Rev. J. S. Ruddach, a son.

In Guildford-street, Russell-square, the wife of the Rev. R. Whittington, a dau.

Dec. 28. At Quarrwood Ryde, Isle of

Some birth announcements from the Gentleman's Magazine, *1868.*

Theoretically, heralds or their deputes were supposed to attend the funerals of all armigers, to marshal and record their heraldry and hatchments and issue **funeral certificates**. Relatively few of these were ever made: some are at the College of Arms and others in the collections of the deputies, such as those made by the Randle Holmeses, now in the Harleian manuscripts in the British Library. Some have been published by county record societies, such as J.P. Rylands (ed.), 'Cheshire and Lancashire funeral certificates, A.D. 1600–1678', *Lancashire and Cheshire Record Society*, 6 (1882).

Occupations

Many aristocratic ancestors, especially girls, were educated at home by private tutors (often clergymen). From the Tudor period onwards it became increasingly common for boys to go to local grammar schools, or boarding schools ('private schools', the best of which are termed 'public schools'). Many such schools have published **lists of alumni** (pupils), usually stating ages and fathers' names, occupations and places of residences.

Boys might then go on to university, either abroad or Oxford and Cambridge, Trinity College Dublin or the Scottish universities, St Andrews, Aberdeen, Glasgow and Edinburgh. Durham was founded in 1832, and since then many more have been established. All the old ones have published alumni lists offering similar information to the school lists.

The Society of Genealogists has a fine collection of alumni volumes and many are now online (at www.archive.org, for example). Often, a whole line of well-off ancestors can be reconstructed using these books alone.

University education was essential to become a clergyman, one of the occupations chosen frequently by younger sons of aristocrats, and their descendants. Church of England clergymen are also traceable through www.theclergydatabase.org.uk/, though bizarrely this leaves out the fathers' names, which are given in the published alumni lists.

Other younger sons, usually also university educated, chose the law. The subject is covered by Mark Herber and Brian Brooks's *My Ancestor was a Lawyer* (2006), and all lawyers are listed in the *Law Lists*, published annually since 1775. **Attorneys at Law** (solicitors) who practised civil law had, from 1728, to qualify by becoming articled clerks, traceable in the indexed 'registers of due execution of clerkship' in The National Archives class KB 170 (1749–1877). These usually state fathers' names. Some lawyers' apprenticeships also appear in the Society of Genealogists' Apprentices' Index (1710–74), available at www.britishorigins.com.

Barristers were lawyers called to practise at the bar through one of the Inns of Court: Lincoln's Inn, Gray's Inn, Middle Temple and Inner Temple (there were also Inns of Chancery: New, Staple, Furnivals, Thavies, Clements, Cliffords, Lyons, Barnards and Sergeants Inns, most of which were eventually absorbed by the main Inns of Court). Many of the admission registers have been published and usually name fathers. Scottish barristers (advocates) are in F.J. Grant, 'The Faculty of Advocates in Scotland, 1532–1943, with genealogical notes', *Scottish Record Society* (1944). Scottish solicitors (called writers to the signet) can be traced through the *Scottish Law List* (published from 1848).

Those barristers who became **judges** are all in E. Foss's *A Biographical Dictionary of the Judges of England from the Conquest to the present time, 1066–1870* (1870).

Many landowners served as **Justices of the Peace** (JPs), who presided over the local Quarter Sessions. They were seldom trained lawyers, so the related records, though interesting for biographical details, will not be much use for piecing together your pedigree. Similarly, other local offices such as Overseers or the Poor and Guardians of the Poor were usually filled by the local great and good.

Parliament was long the preserve of the aristocracy, those with titles sitting in the Lords and their heirs and relations occupying many seats in the Commons. Members are very well chronicled in *The History of Parliament*: see www.historyofparliamentonline.org.

Until the nineteenth century, **medicine** was not considered a respectable profession for younger sons of aristocrats, but it was a resort for those slightly further down the social ladder. The *Medical Directory* was published from 1845 and the *Medical Register* from 1859. These identify the institution where the medic trained, whose records can be examined in turn, and there are good sets at the SoG. After 1815, all apothecaries and many physicians and surgeons who wished to practise in England and Wales were licensed by the Society of Apothecaries. The Society's records are at Guildhall Library, London, indexed in *A list of persons who have obtained certificates of their fitness to practise as apothecaries from August 1, 1815 to July 31, 1840*. Also useful are P.J. and R.V. Wallis' *Eighteenth century medics (subscriptions, licenses, apprenticeships* (1994) and C.H. Talbot and E.A. Hammond's *The medical practitioners in medieval England; a biographical register* (1965).

Those sons who preferred a more active life tended to purchase commissions as **officers** in the army, Royal Navy or, latterly, Royal Air Force. The original records up to the 1920s are at The National Archives (after which they are held by the relevant branch of the armed services). Army officers are listed in the published *Army Lists* (from 1740) and *Navy Lists* (from 1797). For the army, see also 'The Soldier in later Medieval England' project and database (1369–1453) at http://tinyurl.com/kvjyrn; C. Dalton's *English Army Lists and commission registers 1661–1714* (1892–1904) and *George the First's army 1714–1727* (1910–12).

Naval officers are very well served by biographical dictionaries: D. Syrett and R.L. DiNardo's *The Commissioned Sea Officers of the Royal Navy 1660–1815* (1994), J. Charnock's *Biographia Navalis* (1794–8), covering 1660–1798, J. Marshall's *Royal Naval biography* covering those serving in 1823 (1823–35) and W.R. O'Byrne's *A Naval Biographical Dictionary* (1849).

From the seventeenth century to 1848 many men served in the army of the Honourable East India Company (H.E.I.C.), the records of which are housed in the India Office Collection at the British library. At home, men also served in the local militias, whose officers were drawn from the local gentry. They are recorded in militia lists (mostly in The National Archives), though these are generally lacking in much genealogical detail.

Though aristocrats and their descendants are often thought not to have 'sullied their hands with trade', many actually did. The **freedom and burgess rolls** of the towns and cities (usually in local archives) include many upper class people, particularly younger sons who had been apprenticed to town craftsmen. Almost all related records state ages and fathers' names. Many merchants who made their money in the boroughs later bought estates from penniless aristocrats and dragged themselves up into the upper echelons. **Trade directories** record the existence of businesses.

From as early as the seventeenth century, those who had money might deposit it in **bank accounts**. Many records of local banks are found in local archives. Most were swallowed up by larger ones. The Bank of England Archive Section (Threadneedle Street, London, EC2R 8AH, 0207 601 5096, http://tinyurl.com/cpk743n) holds many records of aristocratic ancestors' bank accounts.

Many better off people took out **fire insurance**. Records exist from 1696 onwards, especially the papers of the Sun Fire Office, whose sun plaques are still to be seen on many old buildings. Look in local archives, and also in Guildhall Library, London, for most insurance firms were based in the City.

The *London Gazette* recorded numerous business partnerships, dissolved partnerships and of course **bankruptcies**. *The Times* and local newspapers also tended to cover bankruptcies in detail, often printing inventories of a bankrupt's possessions, which were sold off to try to pay his debts.

Land Holding

Land was the mainstay of the aristocracy and landed gentry. The country was divided into manors, and records of who held them begin, to all practical purposes, with **Domesday Book**. Compiled by the Conqueror in 1086, this recorded who the tenants-in-chief (tenants *in capite*) were in both 1066 and 1086. Domesday Book is published by Phillimore, and much of it is available online at www.domesdaybook.co.uk/. From 1086 to the 1300s, the amount of surviving material on manorial lords is generally rather poor: it is very unusual to find families who can trace their lines back, generation by generation, to someone listed in 1086.

In 1275, Edward I's commissioners compiled the **Ragman Rolls**, recording the rights and liberties granted by himself and his predecessors, and how many of them had been usurped and abused due to his absence on Crusade. The records are in The National Archives (C 47/23). The king then issued the 1278 statute of *Quo Warranto* ('by what right?'), summoning all those who held private franchises and jurisdictions to appear before his judges and show by what right they did so. As many people summoned appealed to precedent, arguing they were only doing what their ancestors had done, these records are a rich source of genealogical information. The records are mostly in The National Archives (class JUST 1), as are the further *Quo Warranto* hearings that were held, ad hoc, until the 1680s.

In Scotland, the term 'Ragman Roll' is applied also to the list of nobles and other subjects superior (tenants-in-chief) who were forced to swear allegiance to Edward I of England during his interference in the Scottish succession in 1291 and 1296. A list of names, published by the Bannatyne Club in 1834, is at http://tinyurl.com/cvsth8y and is extremely useful in identifying early (or the earliest) bearers of family names – names that were often taken from the land families were then holding. Also of interest for this period is the 'Paradox of Scotland' database (www.poms.ac.uk), containing 'all' names found in Scottish charters and other surviving Scottish records from 1093 to 1286.

Generally, the families best recorded in original records are also those most likely to appear in printed pedigrees, but in order to check printed sources, correct mistakes and perhaps prove your ancestor really was a younger son who was missed off the pedigree, the main records to start with are **family muniments** (family papers). If these have survived, they will either be with the head of the family, or in archives: if the latter, they should be listed in the National Register of Archives, www.nationalarchives.gov.uk/nra/default.asp and www.nationalarchives.gov.uk/a2a/ (or www.scan.org.uk/, for Scotland). A fine example of a substantial set of family muniments is the collection of the Dukes of Sutherland, which also has its own website, www.sutherlandcollection.org.uk/places/.

Family muniments may include manorial records; numerous **deeds**, relating to the buying, selling and leasing of land (such as feet of fines); marriage settlements; entails (deeds dictating the descent of land); copies of wills and so on, all good for increasing your knowledge of the family, and full of genealogical information. The have a myriad of uses: I know an aristocrat who is currently studying his family's muniments and is discovering numerous various pieces of land and sources of income which had simply been forgotten about. My *Tracing Your Family History* (2004/2008) explains deeds in detail, and my Scottish and Irish books cover deeds for those countries in detail as well.

Deeds are immensely useful to genealogists, so it is worth investigating those enrolled in **deeds registries**, when they existed. Those concerning land in the East Anglian Fens from 1663 are in Cambridge Record Office. Middlesex land deeds 1709–1938 are in the London Metropolitan Archives. The Deeds Registries for the Yorkshire Ridings, dating from 1704 (West), 1707 (East) and 1735 (North), up to 1970, are at the Northallerton, Beverley and Wakefield record offices respectively. The national **Land Registry** was introduced in 1862, followed by the gradual introduction of compulsory registration of title deeds when property was bought and sold. The Land Registry holds plans and associated records, which can be searched, HM Land Registry, 32 Lincoln's Inn Fields, London, WC2A 3PH, 0207 917 8888, www.landreg.gov.uk.

In Scotland, people holding land direct from the Crown (many of whom were aristocrats) were termed 'subjects superior'. They gained their land by **Crown Charters**, recorded in the records of the Great Seal, Privy Seal and Signatures. Abstracts from the *Registers of the Great Seal of Scotland* (RMS or *Registrum Magni Sigilli Regum Scotorum*) have been published from the start, 1314, up to 1668 (in Latin to 1651): the period to 1919 is covered by manuscript indexes in the National Archives of Scotland (NAS: HM General Register House, 2 Princess Street, Edinburgh, EH1 3YY, www.nas.gov.uk). Retours or **Services of Heirs** allowed and recorded the inheritance of such land by the subject superiors' families. They survive in the Scottish Chancery records, abstracted up to 1700 in three published volumes, *Inquisitionum Retornatarum Abbreviatio*. From 1700 to 1859, there are indexes for each ten years, and from 1860 to the present there are annual indexes (in printed volumes and on CD-ROM from the Scottish Genealogy Society, www.scotsgenealogy.com/). They are often a straightforward way of reconstructing a family line.

Further material on Scots landholding appears in the Register of **Tailzies** (deeds determining the descent of land, indexed 1688–1833 (NAS RT1) and a manuscript index to the 'Register of Entails' 1688–1938 (RT3/1/1-2), both in the National Archives of Scotland. **Sasines**, recording changes in ownership of land, whether by inheritance, sale, mortgage (wadset) or other means, are recorded in registers at the National Archives of Scotland and locally in burgh records.

Ireland's **Deeds Registry**, in Dublin (Registry of Deeds, Henrietta Street, Dublin 1, www.landregistry.ie) has deeds from 1708 and is immensely useful for tracing landholding families.

Another useful Irish source is the **fiants** (*fiant litterae patentes*). These are Chancery warrants concerning the issue of letters patent in Ireland, now lost, but calendared and summarised for 1531–1603 as the *7th–21st Reports of the Deputy Keeper of the Public Records*, and also as *The Irish Fiants of the Tudor Sovereigns During the Reigns of Henry VIII, Edward VI, Philip & Mary, and Elizabeth I* (1994). Those for the reigns of James I and Charles I (1603–49) were calendared by Irish Record Commissioners. Details of many originals are found in the work of pre-1922 genealogists. They include pardons granted to Irish chieftains who submitted to the Tudors in return for their land being granted back to them by the Crown.

Manorial records are concerned with sub-tenants, but most records refer to who the lord was at the time. They are the backbone of the manorial histories in the antiquarian county histories, and the newer *Victoria County History* series.

From the seventeenth century onwards, many landowners 'enclosed' manorial land to create parks and large farms, displacing many peasants from their hereditary holdings, and turning them, involuntarily, into itinerant farm labourers. Some **enclosures** were enacted locally, perhaps only being recorded in the manorial records themselves, but many appear in the records of the Chancery Courts (in The National Archives) and, from the eighteenth century onwards, in private Acts of Parliament (in the Parliamentary Archives).

Historically, payment of tax has been linked closely to possession of land, so landholding aristocrats and gentry appear prominently in all tax lists, starting with Medieval **Lay Subsidies** (taxes paid by the laity, as opposed to the Church). All such national tax lists are at The National Archives and well catalogued at www.nationalarchives.gov.uk/e179/. They include the infamous Ship Money, the raising of which by Charles I was a contributory cause of the Civil War; the **Hearth Taxes** of the 1660s–80s and its equally unpopular successor, the **Window Tax**. **Land Tax** was levied from 1693 to 1963, but with most surviving records from the period 1780–1832. They are arranged by parish within hundreds and list all landholders with property worth 20s or more and (from 1772) tenants, although if more than one tenant lived in a building, only one will be listed. The property may also be described briefly. Returns mainly survive for the country and are in Quarter Session records in county archives. An almost complete record for England and Wales for 1798 is in The National Archives class IR 23. After 1798, the tax could be commuted by a lump-sum payment equivalent to sixteen years' tax. Records of those 'exonerated' are in IR 22. The whereabouts of records can be found in J. Gibson, M. Medlycott and D. Mills' *Land and window tax assessments* (1998).

Then there are the host of other taxes, mostly aimed at transferring money from the coffers of the rich into those of the king. These include taxes on:

Silver plate, 1756–77
Carriages, 1747–87
Male servants, 1777–1852 (except those working in farming, trade or industry). The Society of Genealogists has an index to the employers listed in the 1780 returns.
Game, 1784–1807
Horses used for transport, 1784–1874
Female servants, 1785–92
Coats of arms, 1793–1882
Hair powder, 1795–1861
Dogs, 1796–1882
Empty houses, 1851–1924
Income (for the very wealthy only) 1789, 1803–16 and 1842 to present (the only surviving pre-1842 records are of those who failed to pay).

Extant records list only the tax payers and their survival is very patchy. Some are at The National Archives in classes E 182 and T 47, and many more will be found in county record offices and are always worth searching for. The National Archives of Scotland holds many comparable lists.

These tax lists do not contain genealogical information as such, but by studying a succession of lists, you can see names changing: when

William Biggs stops being listed, he may have died, when Thomas Biggs appears in his place, he may well have been William's son. Some taxes, such as the hearth taxes, provide other information too. Knowing how many hearths were in the family home is an interesting indication of the size of the house, and thus of social status – though grand old medieval houses might actually have had far fewer hearths than the modern, brick-built dwellings of self-made Stuart parvenus. It is salutary to recall that when Winston Churchill was born at Blenheim Palace in 1874, it still only had one bathroom.

David Lloyd George's desire to tax the rich led, in 1910–14, to the creation of his new 'Domesday' survey, the Board of Inland Revenue's **Valuation Office records**. These listed every property in England and Wales, in fascinating detail. The records are in The National Archives (class IR 58) and are described in detail in my *Tracing Your Home's History* (2006) – no use for genealogy, but a fascinating way of learning more about how your family (or your wealthy relatives) lived at the time. Scottish **Valuation Rolls** for 1915 are on www.Scotlands People.gov.uk.

Until the twentieth century, possession of land was also a major qualifier for the right to vote. From 1696 (but mainly from 1711, when they started being deposited with clerks of the peace) until 1872, when secret ballots were introduced, **poll books** were maintained, which listed electors and recorded how they voted, and these can be a useful source of information. Collections are held in local archives, the Society of Genealogists, the British Library and, particularly, the Institute of Historical Research (Senate House, University of London, WC1E 7HU, www.ihrinfo.ac.uk). After 1872 electoral registers were also kept (now mainly held in local archives), which chronicle the growing number of electors as reform eventually led to universal suffrage.

Other Records of the Aristocracy

Besides Burke's and other dedicated genealogical books, the upper classes are well documented in printed sources. These include Walford's *County Families* and the annual volumes of *Who's Who* (a biographical dictionary of the great and good alive at the time) and its supplement volume, the amusingly named *Who was Who* (from 1897) covering people who have died (www.oup.com/whoswho/). *Who's Who* features the great and the good, across the political and military

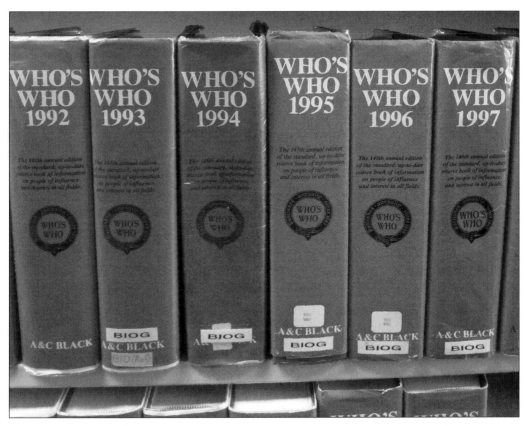

A run of Who's Who *volumes at the Society of Genealogists.*

communities to the business and cultural life of the nation. It began in 1849. It will often supply family details, not always enough for genealogical purposes, but always enough to lead you to the right original records which will tell you more.

Also immensely useful is *The Dictionary of National Biography* (1885), updated as *The Oxford Dictionary of National Biography* (2004) (www.oxforddnb.com). This is not a genealogical work, but it endeavours to provide dates and places of birth/baptism, marriage and death/burial, and the names of the parents, spouse(s) and children. I was one of the writers of the *ODNB*, and where such information was not known, we simply did what we could to research this information, but we were not always successful. The entry for my own ancestor the marine painter Thomas Mitchell (d. 1790) lacks details of his baptism and parents as I have never been able to trace them!

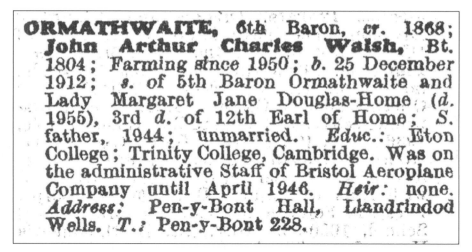

ORMATHWAITE, 6th Baron, cr. 1868; John Arthur Charles Walsh, Bt. 1804; Farming since 1950; b. 25 December 1912; s. of 5th Baron Ormathwaite and Lady Margaret Jane Douglas-Home (d. 1955), 3rd d. of 12th Earl of Home; S. father, 1944; unmarried. Educ.: Eton College; Trinity College, Cambridge. Was on the administrative Staff of Bristol Aeroplane Company until April 1946. Heir: none. Address: Pen-y-Bont Hall, Llandrindod Wells. T.: Pen-y-Bont 228.

A typical entry from Who's Who.

The printed reports of the **Historic Manuscripts Commission** catalogue, and in many cases transcribe, the letters, legal documents and numerous other records of many prominent families. In doing so, they cross-refer to vast numbers of other individuals and families.

The printed **State Papers** (Domestic series and Foreign series: see http://www.british-history.ac.uk/) are a lucky dip of gargantuan proportions, detailing all aspects of the State, and its people, with copious miscellaneous details of the upper classes. So too are the **Acts of the Privy Council** (see http://tinyurl.com/c5sjnsb) and other supplementary volumes such as the *Letters and Papers of the Reign of Henry VIII*, sets of which are in The National Archives and the British Library and many university libraries. For all these, see www.british-history.ac.uk/. The volumes are unlikely to solve a specific genealogical problem (though they might), but it is worth going through the indexes to the volumes to see what appears under your surnames of interest. You never know what new information and clues you will discover.

Equally worth exploring are the printed calendars to the **Close Rolls**, the rolls of 'letters close' issued by the **Court of Chancery**, and the many deeds enrolled within them. The original records are in The National Archives, class C 54. They include **Mortmain** licences – licences to bequeath land to religious bodies or other institutions, from 1279 onwards. The printed calendars to the **Patent Rolls** include grants of land, wardships, offices and nobility. Dating from 1201 to 1945, they represent the longest unbroken archive in the world. The

---

MEMBRANE 36.

Aug. 14. Clarendon.	Licence for Henry de Percy to grant to Henry his son and Mary, daughter of the king's kinsman, Henry, earl of Lancaster, in tail male, the manors of Foston, co. Leicester, and Tadecastre and Pokelynton, co. York, said to be held in chief. **By p.s.**
July 4. York.	Protection with clause *volumus*, until Easter, for Henry de Bello Monte staying in Scotland on the king's service. **By p.s.**
July 31. Windsor.	Ratification of the entry of the abbot and convent of Westminster into the church of Langedon in the diocese of Worcester, which they lately appropriated with the king's licence and by authority of apostolic letters, and of the estate which they have therein, that their possession of the same be not hereafter impeached on the ground that after the appropriation the church became void at a time when the abbey was in the king's hands by the death of the last abbot. **By p.s.**
Sept. 11. Guildford.	Grant to Master John de Salesbury, king's clerk, of the prebend in the church of St. Wolfram, Abbeville, now void by the resignation of John de Wodeford, king's clerk, and in the king's gift in right of his county of Ponthieu and Montreuil. **By p.s.** Mandate in pursuance to the dean and chapter of the said church.
Sept. 12. Guildford.	Licence for Roesia, late the wife of Nicholas Kiriel, tenant in chief, to marry whomsoever she will of the king's allegiance. **By fine of 1 mark.**
Aug. 2. Windsor.	Exemption, for life, of Peter de Seremby from being put on assizes, juries, or recognisances, unless his oath be necessary under the statute, and from appointment as mayor, sheriff, coroner, escheator or other bailiff or minister of the king, against his will. **By p.s.**

This section from the printed Calendars of Patent Rolls for 1334 highlights the range of people and subjects covered by these fascinating records.

originals are in The National Archives, class C 66, and some are online at http://tinyurl.com/6rzdf9c and www.british-history.ac.uk/.

The **Court of Star Chamber**, a sub-'committee' of the Privy Council, ran from 1487 to 1641 and heard cases on many subjects. It is best known for its trials of nobles and others for treason, heresy and rebellion. Surviving records are in The National Archives class STAC and some have been printed in E.L.C. Mullins' *Texts and Calendars, and analytical guide to serial publications* (1958) and Vol. 2, 1957–82 (1983).

On a happier note, many titled families (and some non-titled ones, and some manorial lords and holders of various offices) have hereditary rights to perform certain duties at coronations. The Earls of Loudon, for example, claim the right to carry the Great Spurs, as their ancestors had done since the Middle Ages. G. Woods Wollaston's *Coronation Claims* (1910) provides details of such rights.

The Civil War

Officers and some soldiers on both sides of the *Civil War* appear in pay lists and musters in The National Archives class E 315, but the best resources are published. Sir C. Firth and G. Davies' *The Regimental History of Cromwell's Army* (1940) and E. Peacock's *The army lists of the roundheads and cavaliers* (1874) cover both options well. There is also the 1663 list of Indigent Officers, detailing the claims made by former Royalist officers to the £60,000 bounty that Charles II made available for their relief. This has been published and indexed, with some supplementary information from the Royalist news sheet *Mercurius Aulicus*, the State Papers and other sources, in S. Reid's *Officers and regiments of the Royalist army*, 5 volumes (Partizan Press, n.d.).

Those whom Cromwell's Parliament fined for having fought for Charles I are well documented in Green's *Calendar of the Proceedings of the Committee for Advance of Money, 1642–1656* and *Calendar of the Proceedings of the Committee for Compounding, 1643–1660*. Many officers and men appear in the printed calendars to the Domestic, Thurloe and Clarendon State Papers for this period.

Portraits of Ancestors

Until the development of photography, very few lower class people were recorded in drawings and portraits, but as you go up the social scale, the chances of findings pictures of ancestors increases dramatically, and these are worth trying to track down. The homes of the senior descendants of the families concerned are the best places to start looking. Many collections in private hands and galleries have been catalogued by the Courtauld Institute of Art, Somerset House, Strand, London, WC2R 0RN, www.courtauld.ac.uk.

Have a look too at the National Portrait Gallery, St Martin's Place, London, WC2H 0HE, 0207 306 0055, www.npg.org.uk/search; the National Art Library, Victoria and Albert Museum, Cromwell Road, London, SW7 2RL, 0207 938 8315, www.nal.vam.ac.uk; the Scottish National Portrait Gallery, 1 Queen Street, Edinburgh, EH21JD, http://tinyurl.com/c8r2kbe; and the National Portrait Collection of the National Gallery of Ireland, Merrion Square West, Dublin 2, www.nationalgallery.ie/. It is also worthwhile searching the collection of the National Trust at www.nationaltrustimages.org.uk/.

A miniature portrait of my ancestor Perry Nursey. I found this treasure by tracing a distant cousin who was also descended from Perry Nursey, who happened to have it – and who was kind enough to let me take a digital photograph of it. (Courtesy of Mrs Nancy Bedwell)

Failing these, seek out different descendants of the families concerned, and ask if they have any ancestral portraits: it is not a quick or easy process, but over time, in a piecemeal manner, you will find a lot.

Portraits are particularly useful when trying to work out whether claims of illegitimate descent from aristocrats are true or not. Seeing if pictures of the alleged illegitimate child, or their descendants, look like members of the aristocratic family concerned can be an interesting exercise. It is too easy, of course, to convince yourself of resemblances that are in fact pure coincidence, but if the specific shapes of eyes, eyebrows, lips, noses and ears really match, then you may be onto something. Such inheritance is a matter of genetics, the subject of the next chapter.

Chapter 12

GENETICS AND DNA

G enetics is the new genealogical wonderland, a world out of science fiction, in which so many things that seemed impossible in the past are now possible. If you have aristocratic ancestry, you may be able to use genetics to prove it.

Taking a Test

There are several very good firms, including www.familytreedna.com and www.ethnoancestry.com/, that offer tests. These cost a couple of hundred pounds, and unlock a world of knowledge worth vastly more.

Taking a DNA test is very simple. The genetic testing firm will send you a small brush, like a tooth brush, which you rub inside your cheek, to collect some cells. You have simply to post this back, and they will undertake the necessary tests.

SNPs and STRs

Chromosomes are made of special proteins and DNA, which is composed of many base-pairs of nucleotides, arranged in a double-helix shape. In each human cell is a nucleus, containing twenty-two pairs of chromosomes bearing autosomal DNA, and one pair of chromosomes that include the DNA that determines gender.

The process of myosis generates gametes (eggs in women and sperm in males) and reduces the two sets of chromosomes down to one. During sex, the one set in the sperm combines with the one set in the egg, to create a new, complete set of twenty-three pairs of chromosomes. It is this which generates the next generation.

This complex process causes some slight changes or mutations, called genetic polymorphisms. These include single nucleotide polymorphisms (SNPs) and single tandem repeats (STRs) in the sections of DNA that do not, so far as is known, carry any useful codes needed for creating us.

Individual genes have two or more 'alleles' or possible states of being, usually expressed by scientists as letters, A or T, and C or G. An SNP, also called a 'unique event polymorphism', is a change in a gene's allele, from A to G, for example. Once an SNP has occurred, it will remain unchanged down the generations, so acts as a reliable marker for 'deep ancestry' haplogroup testing.

STRs are rather different, occurring in a different part of the chromosome, and entail a series of multiple alleles or changes caused by the addition or deletion of the number of base-pairs. By counting the base-pairs, geneticists arrive at numerical codes. These mutations occur much more quickly than SNPs, changing over short spans of generations.

The result is two complementary sets of results: SNPs define haplogroups, groups of people who share the same SNP markers, with implied ancestry going back many thousands of years. STRs define much smaller groups of people, related over the last couple of thousand years, or much less. The STR values can often be used to predict haplogroups, though these can only be known for sure through SNP testing.

Male (Y) and Female (mt-DNA) Lines

The randomness of the swapping process caused by myosis means that we generally do not know whether a given gene has come from the mother or the father. There are two exceptions. One is found in the twenty-third pair of chromosomes, which determine gender. This pair can comprise two female or X chromosomes, producing a girl, or an X and a Y chromosome, producing a boy.

When a sperm cell is generated, chance alone determines whether it will receive the male's single X, or single Y chromosome, which it will carry to the waiting egg. It is this random chance that determines the gender of the resulting child. This also means that the Y chromosome in males always comes down from the father, so its route down the generations can be extrapolated back. Each Y chromosome has travelled down the direct male line, father to son, since about 1,200 million years ago, when sexual reproduction began amongst our single-celled ancestors in Earth's primeval oceans.

Y chromosome tests can therefore be performed on males alone. Women wishing to know their male-line inheritance must have a test performed on their father, or a male-line relative of their father's, such as one of his sons or brothers.

The other sort of test is on the mitochondrial DNA (mt-DNA) inside the ovum, which passes down from mothers to their children, but which only their daughters will transmit to their own offspring. It is thus a certain marker of the female line, the mother's mother's mother's line, of families.

Once an SNP mutation has arisen, either in the Y chromosome or the mitochondrial DNA, it is passed on from generation to generation: whoever has such a mutation belongs to an identifiable group, termed a 'clade' or 'haplogroup'. When a further mutation occurs in a member of a haplogroup, it is passed down as well, so this defines a new haplogroup (which one can also term a sub-haplogroup) within the existing haplogroup. Further mutations within that group define new haplogroups (or sub-sub-haplogroups, though such terms are rarely employed), and so on. Although such mutations have no discernible effect on appearance or behaviour, the simple possession of such mutations can be used, in purely genetic terms, to define peoples and perhaps even races.

On a much closer genealogical level, STRs in the male-line, Y chromosome (but not the female-line mitochondria) can also be used to 'fine tune' the distinctions and similarities between men to within very close degrees of cousinship.

Practical Application: SNPs

Genetic testing (either on yourself or, if you are a woman, on a close male-line relative, such as your father, brother, etc.), will establish your male-line (Y chromosome) haplogroup, and your female-line (mt-DNA) haplogroup.

Immediately, this hurtles you back thousands of years up your family tree, to the time of the earliest aristocrats and kings, and then much further back into human history. 'Aristocracy' means 'rule by the best'. For most of our history as humans, we lived in small bands of hunter-gatherers. Only the fittest and most able survived. In each band, the best of these became the natural leader. Each generation entailed a brutal honing of our genes, eliminating all but the best. In a very real sense, *all* human ancestry before 10,000 years ago, as revealed by genetics, is 'aristocratic'.

Each haplogroup has its story. In the male line, A and B are the oldest, most commonly found in Africa, where our species evolved. The originator of A, who is the male-line ancestor of all humans alive now, was one man, who probably lived about 80,000 years ago, almost certainly in East Africa. He has been nicknamed the 'Genetic Adam'. The rest of the groups descend from the small group or groups of humans who left Africa and slowly colonised the rest of the world. The group 'IJK' were the first modern humans to enter Europe, about 40,000 years ago. The commonest in Western Europe now, however, is their descendant R, which spread with Neolithic farmers, from about 4,000 BC onwards.

Each haplogroup has an equally branching family tree of sub-groups, identified R1, R2, etc., and then R1a, R1b, and so on. The commonest sub-group in Europe is actually R1b1a2a1a1 (identified by the markers L11 and S217). Its discoverer, Dr Jim Wilson, nicknamed it 'The Atlantic Modal Haplotype'. There has been a strong warrior element in its spread, and the spread of its own sub-groups, over the last 2,500 years, resulting in some sub-groups dominating wide areas, to the almost complete exclusion of others. R1b1a2a1ab4b (M 222), for example, identifies the sub-group of the Ui Neill in northern and western Ireland. Anyone with that marker is related, somehow, to the

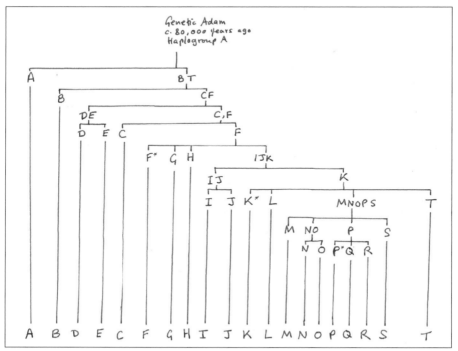

This chart shows how the different Y chromosome haplogroups identified by geneticists link up and form a spreading family tree of the human race, as defined by male-line genetic signatures.

119

High King Niall of the Nine Hostages. George Washington, First President of the United States, belonged to this male-line lineage: had he been tested, the result should have shown him carrying the M 222 marker distinctive of this branch. The Irish story is recounted with brilliant clarity on John D. McLaughlin's website at http://clanmaclochlainn.com/dna.htm.

A similar story unfolds for the female (mt-DNA) lines, also (confusingly) identified by letters of the alphabet, though as these mutate more slowly, the results are less detailed in terms of sub-groups. All lines go back to a woman who lived in East Africa about 140,000 years ago, dubbed the 'Mitochondrial Eve'. She had many descendants, both male and female (but only her descendant the 'Genetic Adam' left any *male*-line descendants who are alive today).

Over a decade ago Professor Sykes identified the seven commonest female lineages in Europe, X, U, K, H, V, J and T, and nicknamed them 'the Seven Daughters of Eve'. All were here during the Ice Age, except perhaps T, which arrived about 11,000 years ago. About 45 per cent of all Europeans belong, in the female line, to H.

Simply knowing your haplogroup can enable you to establish cousinships, albeit probably *very* distant ones, to aristocracy and royalty. Some are listed at www.isogg.org/famousdna.htm. Queen Victoria and Marie Antoinette both belonged to the female-line haplogroup H, for example, and Genghis Khan was male-line haplogroup C. Some will object that describing relationships based on haplogroups is ridiculously generalised: maybe so, but if you belong to female-line haplogroup H (and almost half of us in the West do) then the fact is that the mitochondrial DNA in each cell of your body, and the mitochondrial DNA in the cells of Queen Victoria, came down, generation by generation, from the *same* Ice Age woman. However distant, you and Queen Victoria are cousins, and that's that.

Genetics works by comparison with others. If you are a Muggins, and think you have a family connection with the Muggins Dukes of Muggins, then discovering whether you and the present duke, or one of his male-line relatives, belong to the same male-line sub-haplogroup will indicate you are working along the right lines.

Just as women wanting to learn about their own male line need to find a male-line relative to have a test for them, so do we all need to find 'substitutes', depending on which lines we want to investigate. If I want to explore my mother's male line, i.e., the male line of my maternal grandfather, I must obtain a sample from my maternal

Adam and Eve being expelled from Eden, carving from Fontevraud Abbey, France.

grandfather himself, or one of his sons, or one of their sons, or even one of his brother's sons.

Practical Application: STRs

Knowing your sub-group in the great, branching family tree of humans helps establish your general 'racial' background up that line, and indicates the broad group of families to which you are distantly related. Now it is time to use STRs to 'fine tune' your knowledge. Within each male-line (Y) sub-haplogroup, the myriad smaller sub-branches are identifiable through STR results. Because STRs mutate so frequently, it is sometimes possible to tell quite close cousins apart by this means. Within one family, STR results can even identify different branches and sub-branches.

The genetic profiles of many surnames are being studied actively. The best collection of projects is at www.familytreedna.com/projects.aspx.

If you believe, for example, that your Muggins line branched off the main stem of the Dukes of Muggins, you can try a comparative test with a ducal Muggins. If your STR results match up exactly, then you are probably right. One or two differences in a test on 67 or (better still) 111 markers may be explicable if a couple of centuries have elapsed: one would expect a few mutations to have taken place in that period of time. More than two or three differences, however, may suggest the connection was much further back than you thought. Yet more differences suggest your theory is simply wrong.

This sort of testing has exciting potential if you think your ancestor was the illegitimate offspring of someone aristocratic or royal. Genes simply do not care whether couples were married or not. If Mr Smith shares the same STR results as the Duke of Muggins, then either a previous Duchess of Muggins had an affair with a Mr Smith, resulting in the ducal line of Muggins actually having Smith genes, or a previous Duke of Muggins made a Miss Smith pregnant and produced an illegitimate offspring, surnamed Smith, but actually of male-line, Muggins ancestry. If Mr Smith suspects the latter, and has a comparative test with the Duke of Muggins, and their STR results match, then he has effectively proved his case.

I have seen this work, time and again, in real life. Nicholas Green had a persistent family tradition that his illegitimate Green ancestor had been fathered by 'the lord of the manor'. Genealogical research suggested that the culprit could have been a nineteenth-century army major, George Betts of Wortham Hall. Pictures of the people concerned showed striking similarities, but there were absolutely no documents to prove the connection for certain. Mr Green might have spent the rest of his life wondering, but a test on his Y chromosomes and those of a legitimate descendant of Major Betts showed that they matched *exactly*. Much encouraged, and with considerable justification, he has changed his name to Nicholas Betts-Green.

Autosomal DNA

Such a triumph would not have worked had Mr Green's illegitimate ancestor been a girl, for she would not have carried her father's tell-tale, male-line Betts Y chromosome. However, since 2010, a new type of test has appeared: autosomal DNA testing. Each firm has a different name for it: www.familytreedna.com call it 'Family Finder'.

Autosomal tests do not look at specific chromosomes. Instead, they look at all your genes, and see how many you have in common with others who have also been tested. They are so accurate that they can predict whether you and someone else are fourth, third, second or first cousins, or even siblings (but further back than fourth cousins, they lose definition rapidly). Such a test will not tell you by which part of your family tree you are related to someone else: it will say 'you are this person's second cousin . . .' but it will not say 'the connection is through your father's mother'. That part is for you to attempt to puzzle out using genealogical records.

The test works best when you have a comparative test with some-one who you think is your relative up to the degree of about fourth cousinship. The test results will simply say whether you are related or not. Thus, if you think your grandmother was the illegitimate child of the Duke of Muggins, and an autosomal DNA test with the current duke confirms that you are his second cousin, then you will know your theory must be right.

Negative Results

Like the oracle at Delphi, genetic test results depend on asking the right question, and interpreting the results correctly. Negative results – the lack of a match between two people who were thought to be related, does not always mean that a theory is wrong. Perhaps you think your ancestor was the illegitimate son of a Muggins Duke of Muggins, but a test between you and the present duke does not show a match. It may mean that your theory is wrong. However, it may be that you are right, but that one of the lines was broken at a different point. Maybe, for example, the present duke was conceived through a secret affair of the duke's mother, so he lacks the identifying Muggins genes for which you were hoping. In that case, it would be this factor, and not a fault in your theory, which would account for you and the duke having different DNA profiles. Further tests, with other relatives of the duke's, who do carry the Muggins family's distinctive DNA, may produce a match with you after all.

Ötzi the Iceman

One way by which I have learned about genetics is to have tests undertaken on myself, and then to do as much as I could to understand them and explore their ramifications. The first test I had, a few years ago, informed me that I belonged to a male-line haplogroup, G, which is very rare in Europe, but is very common in Turkey and Armenia. I assumed this meant my ancestors had come to Germany (and thence to England) from Turkey fairly recently. However, DNA technology is advancing so rapidly that, when I had another test done a few years later, I obtained far more detail. Just as each haplogroup fits into a single, branching family tree of humanity, as defined by male-line descent, so too does each haplogroup have its own, branching family tree, defined by SNP markers – and new makers are being sought and discovered all the time. So now, the G haplogroup has its own, branching family tree, and I know to which branch I belong – it is coded G2a and is defined by the marker P15, which appears in my Y chromosome. Then, G2a itself branches, and I come from G2a3b1a, identified by the marker L140. Everyone with the marker L140 also has the marker P15, but by far from everyone with P15 has L140, so we know L140 must be a sub-group of P15 – or, in genealogical terms, the progenitor of the L140 group must have been descended from the progenitor of the P15 group.

It is like saying that the Fortescues of Dorset were descended from the Fortescues of Norfolk, only with genetic markers in place of haplogroups, and much, much greater timescales. When and where these progenitors lived is a matter of speculation based on where people

Ötzi the Iceman.

bearing the identifying markers are now. Most men who have the L140 marker are also of northern European origin: one of them, by complete coincidence, is Dr Geoff Swinfield, one of the people who taught me to be a genealogist.

It is thought likely that our ancestor lived in northern Europe, about 3,000 years ago. His forebears must have come from the Middle East, where the G haplotype is most common. A clue to when our ancestors may have arrived comes from a body found frozen solid in the Alps. It is of a man, clothed in well-tailored animal furs, who died about 5,300 years ago, and who was carrying with him some copper – the first worked metal ever found in northern Europe. He has been nicknamed 'Ötzi the Iceman'.

Recently, his genes were analysed, and he was found to be G2a4 (marker L91). He was not my ancestor, but his forebears must have been closely related to my G2a3 ancestors. Were he and my ancestors part of a north-westward movement of people who had inherited the craft of metalworking from their own Middle Eastern ancestors? Maybe, maybe not – it is interesting to speculate. But what is beyond doubt is that, 5,300 years ago, Ötzi and my direct male-line ancestors were close cousins, and he belongs to my family tree.

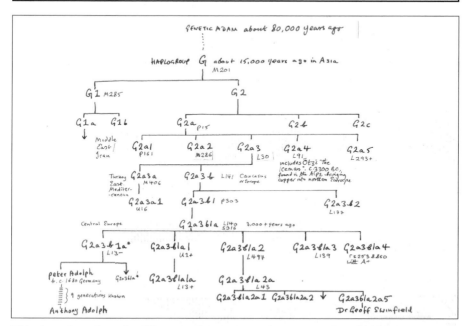

This chart shows how the different Y chromosome sub-groups within Haplogroup G link up and form a spreading family tree of this sub-set of the human family, as defined by male-line genetic signatures.

Genetics Versus Records

DNA testing has its limits. If you think a female ancestress was the illegitimate child of a duke right back in the seventeenth century, then no amount of genetic testing is likely to help you. But used intelligently and creatively, genetic testing can often tell you an enormous amount about your origins which you could not have known otherwise. It can often be used to prove connections – to aristocrats, or to anyone – that could never have been proved using paper-based research.

Further Reading
This subject is carefully explained in Debbie Kennett's *DNA and Social Networking* (2011), in the writings of Chris Pomery (www.dnaand familyhistory.com/) and also on the website of the International Society of Genetic Genealogy, www.isogg.org.

Chapter 13

ROUTES TO ROYALTY

A Bond with Time

When I was young, I used to think that the greatest appeal of genealogy lay in the way it connects us to other people. When I was older, and travelling around Britain making television programmes about family history, I thought that the main attraction of genealogy was the way it could connect us to places. Yet now that I am older still, I have become convinced that genealogy serves us most powerfully through the bond it creates between us and time.

All views are correct. In the case of aristocratic ancestors, genealogy can forge fascinating links between yourself and aristocrats, and lead to much enjoyable communication between you and them. When genealogy links you back to the ancestral home of an aristocratic ancestor, the length of time the family has been there and the many, varied, connections between ancestors and the land are easy to discover and can stir the soul. To survey the very fields your noble forebears were farming when Coeur de Lion set out for the Crusades, and to stand amongst a set of church brasses, knowing that your origins are as deeply entwined with them as the ivy that cloaks the belfry, can be deeply moving.

A row of churchyard tombs stretching back into the past deepens the links between land and time, but ultimately we know there must have been an occasion when the ancestors first arrived on the land, whether they were Normans, granted the estate by the Conqueror himself, or Saxons who had been there since their people came over from Germany – or further back still. In *Puck of Pook's Hill* (1906), Kipling fantasises about the Hobden family's connections back to Roman times:

When Julius Fabricius, Sub-Prefect of the Weald,
In the days of Diocletian owned our Lower River-field,
He called to him Hobdenius – a Briton of the Clay,
Saying: 'What about that River-piece for layin' in to hay?
. . .

His dead are in the churchyard – thirty generations laid.
Their names were old in history when Domesday Book was made.
And the passion and the piety and prowess of his line
Have seeded, rooted, fruited in some land the Law calls mine.

Perhaps there really are some families still living on the land their ancestors farmed in Roman times: some farmers along Hadrian's Wall claim descent from the last centurions posted there to guard its towers. But, parts of Scotland and Ireland aside, most of the families who ended up as the aristocratic proprietors of the land were descended from incoming conquerors, not native farmers.

But as long as you can trace the lines back, it does not matter, ultimately, where your forebears lived. The bond with time that long genealogies create is portable, and remains intact, regardless of the wanderings of your distant forebears. This is where aristocratic ancestors serve our psychological needs so well, because through their intermarriages they connect us back to ever older families, and may ultimately allow us to trace back to royalty.

Royal pedigrees can go back a very long time indeed, far further than any others, partly because many of them are genuinely very old, and partly because, in most settled, farming societies, royal pedigrees have long been an important tool in the pact between humanity and time. In the ancient world, the passage of time was marked, not by numbered years, but by counting the regnal years of each monarch. Although we now have a sophisticated method of numbering our years, we still refer, habitually, to the nineteenth century as 'Victorian', the eighteenth as 'Georgian', and so on.

It is through connecting back, via aristocratic ancestors, to royal pedigrees, that we can trace genealogical lines as far back as any human genealogical line can go, and thus root ourselves, as deeply as possible, within the passage of time itself.

The British Royal Family

Charles, Prince of Wales, and his son and heir Prince William the Duke of Cambridge, are descended in the male line (through Prince Phillip) from the Greek royal family, who came from the Danish House of Oldenbourg.

Queen Elizabeth II and her predecessors inherited the throne through the family of Queen Victoria: the male line goes back through

Victoria's husband Prince Albert of Saxe-Coburg-Gotha, which was originally the House of Wettin, traceable back to Dietrich I, Count of Hassegau (d. 982), who claimed descent from a tribal chieftain, Widukind, in the AD 700s.

Victoria was the last monarch of the House of Hanover, which ruled in Britain through its descent from the marriage of Ernst Augustus of Hanover and Sophia of the Palatine in 1659. The Hanovers go back to the old German House of Este in Italy, whose earliest certain ancestor was Adalbert d'Este in the AD 900s.

Sophia's father was the ill-starred Frederick V of the Palatine (Bavaria) of the House of Wittlesbach, a male-line descendant of Berthold, Margrave in Bavaria (d. 980). Sophia's mother was Elizabeth Stuart, sister of Charles I. Their father was James VI of Scots (d. 1625), who became James I of England in 1603, when he inherited the English throne. His claim was through his great-grandmother Margaret Tudor, wife of James IV Stuart, King of Scots and daughter of Henry VII. In the interim, England had been ruled by Margaret's brother Henry VIII and his children, Edward VI, 'Bloody' Mary and Elizabeth I (d. 1603).

Henry VII, the first Tudor king, won his throne at the Battle of Bosworth in 1485. His male line, short and undistinguished, was falsely connected back, at Henry's behest, to the Welsh princes, and thence to their mythical ancestor, Brutus of Troy. But Henry VII's genealogical claim to the throne was via his mother Margaret Plantagenet, daughter of John Beaufort, Duke of Somerset, a grandson of John of Gaunt, son of Edward III, of the house of Plantagenet.

The Plantagenets gained their name from their use of a sprig of yellow-flowered broom, the *planta genista*, as their emblem. Henry II (1154–89), the first Plantagenet king, was the son of Geoffrey Count of Anjou, whose Anjouvin ancestry goes back to Fulk IV le Réchin, Count of Anjou, son of Geoffrey II Count of Gâtinais and his wife Ermengarde, daughter of Fulk III Nerra of Anjou, descended in the male line from Ingeler of Anjou, son of Tortulf the Woodman, son of Torquat who was born in the late AD 700s.

Henry II's mother Maud was the daughter of Henry I, son of William the Conqueror. William's great-great-great-grandfather Rollo (d. 932), also called 'Hrolf the Ganger', was a Viking or 'Northman' who conquered the part of northern France that became known as Normandy. Dudo of Saint-Quentin's *Norman Chronicle* (*c.* AD 966) mythologised Rollo as an Aeneas-like hero, descended from the Trojans, who founded Rouen as a new Troy in the north. In fact, Rollo was probably a younger son of Ragnvald, Jarl (earl) of Orkney (d. AD 894), who was also Jarl of Möre, Norway, a great-grandson of Halfdan Gamle, 'the stingy', King in Vestfold. Halfdan was ancestor of the Norwegian kings, and was descended from an ancient line of sacred kings seated at Uppsala, for whom descent was claimed from the goddess Freya.

William the Conqueror's wife Matilda was daughter of Baldwin V, Count of Flanders (d. 1067). Baldwin's great-great-great-grandfather Baldwin II (d. 918) was son of Judith, daughter of Charles the Bald (d. 877), a grandson of the great Holy Roman Emperor Charlemagne (d. 814).

Charlemagne (d. AD 814), the first Holy Roman Emperor, to whom a vast number of aristocratic and royal lines can be traced back.

Those are the main royal stems to which people with royal British ancestry can connect, depending of course on how far back your ancestor branched off. There are many more: further lines and ancestors derived from this main stem will be explored in the next chapters.

Tudor Ancestry

Sometimes, you have to work hard to find your Welsh ancestry. Other times, someone has done the work for you. A gravestone in the cemetery in Cranbrook Road, Tenterden, Kent, reads:

In Honour of the memory of John Hay-Edwards formerly of Westwell, Tenterden, lineal descendant of Iddon of Dudleston, who was brother of Tudor progenitor of the Tudor Dynasty (their common ancestor being Tudor of Trefor circa 636) through Thomas Edwards of Kilhendre, Dudleston and of Grete Manor, Salop, first baronet 1644, who with his grandfather Hugo Edwards joint founder of the Shrewsbury School 1551 lies buried in the lady Chapel St Chads Old Church of that town. Died on the 9th January 1929.

Books Chronicling Royal Ancestry

A very detailed and accurate genealogical account of the British royal family appears at the beginning of the 1965 edition of *Burke's Peerage*.

You can enter an eighteenth-century wonderland through the pages of William Betham's *Genealogical Tables of the Sovereigns of the World* (1795) and James Anderson's *Royal genealogies, or the genealogical tables of Emperors, Kings and Princes, from Adam to these times* (1732, 2nd edn 1736). The latter's subtitle says it all: *Part 1 Begins with a chronological history of the world from the beginning of time to the Christian era, and then the genealogies of the earliest great families* [including the Biblical genealogies] *and most ancient sovereigns of Asia, Europe, Africa and America, down to Charlemain, and many of 'em down to these times. Part 2, Begins with the Grand Revolution of Charlemain, and carries on the Royal and princely Genealogies of Europe down to these times; concluding with those of the Britannic Isles.*

More contemporary is *Burke's Royal Families of the World: Europe and Latin America*, Vol. 1 (1977, a new edition, just covering Europe and edited by William Bortrick, is due to be published in 2013).

Jiří Louda and Michael MacLagan's beautifully illustrated *Lines of Succession: heraldry of the Royal Families of Europe* (1981) is well worth exploring. David Williamson's *Brewer's British Royalty* (1996) includes pedigrees for all the British lines, including the Saxons, Scots and Welsh princes, the latter based in part on the work of Patrick Montague-Smith.

W.H. Turton's *The Plantagenet Ancestry* shows over 7,000 ancestors of Elizabeth Plantagenet, daughter of Edward IV (and wife of Henry VII). Gerald Paget's *The Lineage and Ancestry of H.R.H. Charles, Prince of Wales,* 2 vols (1977) covers a yet vaster collection of royal and aristocratic ancestors.

Gateway Ancestors

In reality, very few aristocratic male lines lead back to royalty. Most lead to dead ends, untraced back before the family gained its title. You may be able to trace them further back using normal genealogical sources, but such lines are unlikely to lead to royalty. Instead, once you have found aristocratic ancestors, you need to start exploring *all* their lines of ancestry, using printed sources such as *Burke's Peerage*, looking up the wives' lines as well as the husbands', exploring all four grandparents, eight great-grandparents, and so on. As you trace these back, you are likely to find one or two rising up the social scale, and at some point you may find one line leading back to royalty.

There is a reason for this. Medieval royalty was not as endogamous as their successors from the seventeenth century onwards: sometimes they did marry into other royal families, but often they chose wives and sons-in-law from amongst their nobles. This practice was particularly pronounced from the time of Edward III onwards, when his many offspring and their descendants formed rival factions, whose squabbling resulted in the Wars of the Roses (1455–85). The web of marriage alliances formed by those factions stretched right across the aristocracy, each side marrying into other aristocratic families so as to form alliances and build up power bases.

The result was that an enormous dose of blue blood came gushing down into the aristocracy, and was quickly disseminated further into the ranks of the gentry. The particular portals through which it flowed are sometimes termed 'Gateway Ancestors'. It's a necessarily vague term, because of course anybody who has a child is a 'gateway': all their ancestors automatically become the ancestors of that child and their descendants too. But if you find such a Gateway Ancestor, who had royal blood in their veins, then their royal ancestors are yours as well.

Gateway Ancestors have a particular resonance in America. Amongst the shipfuls of early colonists were a fair number of sons of gentry or aristocratic families with ancestry going back to the Plantagenets. There were also families of blue-blooded aristocrats who married into early colonising families: Frances, Arabella and Susan, three daughters of Thomas Clinton, 3rd Earl of Lincoln, descended from the Blessed Margaret Pole, last of the Plantegents, married respectively to John, son of Sir Ferdinando Gorges, proprietor of Maine; Isaac Johnson, a New England settler and John Humphrey, Deputy Governor of Massachusetts, for example.

The genealogy of colonies works in a strange way. Each time a new wave of settlers arrives, they or their children or grandchildren tend to marry into families descended from the earlier waves. As time passes, the new country's population grows vastly bigger than it was at first, but however enormous it becomes, most of the population have bloodlines going back to the original, tiny population of settlers. Huntingdon's Disease is widespread amongst the Afrikaaners in South Africa because one of the early settlers just happened to be a carrier. Because there was some royal blood amongst the early pioneers of America, a huge swathe (if not actually all) of the modern North American population have Gateway Ancestors leading back to English royalty.

The phenomenon is displayed most clearly through studies of the American presidents, virtually all of whom can be traced back to a Gateway Ancestor. Thus, we can trace the first President, George Washington back through the Reade, Windebank, Dymoke, Talboys and Gascoigne to the marriage of Sir John Neville (son of Warwick 'The Kingmaker') and Elizabeth Holland, both of whom had Plantagenet ancestry. To this stem we can attach the Rootes ancestry of the Second World War American general George Smith Patton, whilst from the Kingmaker's sister Lucy, who married Sir Anthony Browne, a line comes down to Franklin Delano Roosevelt, and the same exercise can be repeated for almost all the others: the Bushes were particularly well endowed with lines back to royalty. See *Burke's Presidential Families of the USA* (1975/1981) and Hugh Brogan and Charles Mosley's *American Presidential Families* (1993).

The subject of Gateway Ancestors had been researched extensively on both sides of the Atlantic. The best place to start is the Marquis of Ruvigny and Raineval's *The Blood Royal of Great Britain, being a roll of the living descendants of Edward IV and Henry VII* (1903) and *The Plantagenet roll of the blood royal, being a complete table of all the descendants now living of Edward III, King of England*, which is published in four volumes: *Clarence, Exeter, Essex and Mortimer-Percy*, describing the descendants of George Duke of Clarence, Anne Duchess of Exeter, Isabel Countess of Essex and Lady Elizabeth Percy, formerly Mortimer.

The books start with a series of printed family trees coming down from the royal family, and are then continued by narrative pedigrees in the style of Burke's. Some are available online (at Ancestry.co.uk, for example), but because of the need to refer back to the tables, and to the index at the back, a printed copy in a library is considerably easier to use.

Ruvigny enumerated only about 20,000 living descendants of the Plantagenets, because (as he realised) he relied on printed sources that left out most junior lines of families. The true number of descendants, including all the younger children and their progeny, runs to many millions.

Ruvigny was a staunch Jacobite, who believed that the senior heir of the deposed James II was the rightful ruler of Britain. To try to subvert Edward VII's possession of the throne, he sought to trace as many lines as he could down from the later Plantagenets, mainly to show how many were *senior* to King Edward. But regardless of Ruvigny's aims, the result was an extremely interesting series of reference books – and in many ways, instead of undermining Edward and his heirs, he reminds us all of the extent to which our present Queen and her family sit right at the very heart of a vast, densely interconnected web of families that extends, ultimately, to encompass almost the entirety of her subjects.

Back in 1848 (and running to several editions), Burke's published *The Royal Families of England, Scotland, and Wales, with their descendants*, a series of charts showing the royal ancestry of selected families – and largely reliant, of course, on those families and their relations buying copies, that they could leave nonchalantly lying about, open on the right page, for their guests to notice and be impressed by. It appeared in several revised editions, as *Royal Descents and Pedigrees of Founders' Kin*.

Joseph Foster produced several beautifully decorated volumes on the same theme, *Our Noble and Gentle Families of Royal Descent* (1883 and 1885) and *The Royal Lineage of Our Noble and Gentle Families* (1884, 1886 and 1887). Charles Mosley's *Blood Royal: From the time of Alexander the Great to Queen Elizabeth II* (2002) besides being a fascinating account

PEDIGREE CXXXVI. **Robert Mitford, Esq.**

Edward I. King of England, *d.* 7 July, = Eleanor, dau. of Ferdinand III. King of
1307. Castile.

The Princess Elizabeth, dau. of Edward I. = Humphrey de Bohun, Earl of Hereford and
and widow of John, Earl of Holland, Essex, slain at Boroughbridge, 1321.

William de Bohun, Earl of Northampton, = Elizabeth, dau. of Bartholomew de Badles-
K.G., *d.* in 1360. mere, and widow of Edmund Mortimer.

Lady Elizabeth, dau. of William de Bohun, = Richard Fitzalan, Earl of Arundel, beheaded
Earl of Northampton, K.G. 21 Richard II.

Thomas, Lord = Lady Elizabeth Fitzalan, = Sir Robert Goushill, Knt. of Heveringham.
Mowbray, Earl dau and coheir of Richard,
Marshal. Earl of Surrey.

Joan, dau. and coheir of Sir Robert Goushill, = Thomas, Lord Stanley, K.G., *d.* in 1458-9.
of Heveringham.

Sir William Stanley, K.G., of Holt, (2nd son of Thomas, Lord Stanley,)
Chamberlain to HENRY VII.

Jane, dau. of Sir William Stanley, K.G. = Sir John Warburton, of Warburton and
Arley, Knight of the body to Henry VII.,
d. 15 Henry VIII.

Sir Piers Warburton, Knt. of Warburton and = Elizabeth, dau. and eventual heiress of Rich-
Arley, eldest son, *d.* 5 June, 4 Edward VI. ard Winnington, of Winnington.

Jane, eldest dau. of Sir Piers Warburton, = Sir William Brereton, Knt. of Brereton, bur.
Knt. there, 4 Sept. 1559.

Elizabeth, dau. of Sir William Brereton, = Thomas Venables, Esq., Baron of Kinderton,
Knt., *d.* June, 1591, bur. at Meddlewich. *d.* 8 Dec. 1606, *Inq. p. m.*, 4 Jac.

Mary, dau. of Thomas Venables, Baron of = Richard Assheton, Esq. of Middleton, co.
Kinderton. Lancaster.

Ralph Assheton, Esq. of Middleton, M.P. = Elizabeth, dau. of John Kaye, Esq., of
for Cheshire, *d.* 17 Feb. 1650. Woodsome.

Sir Ralph Assheton, Bart. of Middleton, so = Anne, dau. of Sir Ralph Assheton, Bart. of
created 17 Aug. 1660. Whalley Abbey, co. Lancaster.

John Assheton, Esq. of Burn, co. York, 2nd son of Sir Ralph Assheton, Bart. of Middleton.

Anne Assheton, eldest dau. and coheir. = Robert Mitford, Esq. of Mitford Castle, *b.*
1662, High Sheriff of Northumberland, 1697.

Robert Mitford, Esq. of Mitford Castle, High = Mary, dau. of Sir Richard Osbaldeston, Knt.
Sheriff in 1723, *b.* 8 Aug. 1686, *d.* 20 July, of Hunmanby, co. York.
1756.

Robert Mitford, Esq. of Mitford Castle, *b.* = Anne, dau. of John Lewis, Esq. of Jamaica.
1718, *d.* 1784.

Bertram Mitford, Esq. of Mitford Castle, *b.* = Tabitha, dau. of Francis Johnson, Esq.,
1749, *d.* in May, 1800. M.D., of Newcastle.

Robert Mitford, Esq. of Mitford Castle, = Margaret, dau. of James Dunsmure, Esq.
Rear Admiral, R.N., *b.* 26 Jan. 1781 ; 19th
in direct descent from EDWARD I. King of
England.

An example of a royal descent from Burke's The Royal Families of England, Scotland, *and Wales.*

of royal genealogy, also notices many lines coming down to other families.

There are many American books on Gateway Ancestors. All have much content that is useful and interesting for British readers. They include Gary Boyd Roberts's *Ancestors of American Presidents* (1995), *Notable Kin* (1998, 1999), *The Royal Descents of 600 Immigrants to the American Colonies or the United States* (2004, 2008); A. Adams and H.H. d'Angerville's *Living Descendants of Blood Royal* (1959); David Faris's *Plantagenet Ancestry of Seventeenth Century Colonists* (1996, 1999); Frederick L. Weis' *The Magna Charta Sureties, 1215* (1991, 1999) and his *Ancestral Roots of Certain American Colonists* (1992, 2004).

So numerous are the Emperor Charlemagne's bloodlines in Britain, France and Germany, that he can fairly be claimed as ancestor of all of Europe: via Gateway Ancestors, he is ancestor of innumerable Americans as well. In America, organisations such as Order of the Crown of Charlemagne (http://charlemagne.org/) and The Society of the Descendants of Charlemagne (http://tinyurl.com/cdd92pk) act both as genealogical societies and social clubs. Some of their publications are in the Society of Genealogists, such as A.L. Langston and J. Orton Buck's *Pedigrees of Some of the Emperor Charlemagne's Descendants* (1974).

Illegitimate Descents

We must all have numerous ancestors who were the illegitimate offspring of aristocratic and royal dynasties. *Droit du seigneur* (the right of feudal lords to sleep with brides on their wedding nights), never existed as an established law in Europe, but it is self-evident that powerful feudal lords could force their tenants' wives or daughters to sleep with them: probably, many did, and the poor fathers and husbands seldom dared do anything about it.

Descent from aristocracy is an easy origin to claim for any illegitimate ancestor, or for any ancestor whose real origins cannot be traced, but in some (or many?) cases, it may actually be true. Genetic testing may now prove such connections: otherwise, such descents can only usually be proved if the aristocratic father acknowledged his illegitimate progeny, either openly or tacitly, by being the child's godfather (a fact that may or may not be recorded in a parish register) and/or leaving the child or its mother money in his will.

Most illegitimate descents from the casual affairs of royalty have probably gone unrecorded. Those that are known about, and are

Filming Granada TV's In Search of Lost Royals, *about the descendants of royal bastards, at the College of Arms, with former royal correspondent Jennie Bond and Thomas Woodcock, Garter Principal King of Arms.*

widely accepted, are chronicled in Chris Given-Wilson and Alice Curteis' *The Royal Bastards of Medieval England* (1984), concerned with the medieval period; Peter Beauclerk-Dewar and R. Powell's *Right Royal Bastards: the fruits of passion* (2006), which brings the story down to two alleged sons of Edward VIII; and Anthony Camp's *Royal Mistresses and Bastards: fact and fiction, 1714–1936* (2007).

Sometimes, the memory of an ancestor working for the royal family might spark the family fantasy of a royal liaison: or maybe there really was one. Royal Household Staff Lists, covering all the royal palaces 1660–1924, from 'Chocolate Maker to the Queen' to moletaker, are at Windsor Castle's Archives and can also be searched at http://tinyurl.com/buzt8dh.

What are the Implications?

One way or another, we are all descended from royalty. Many people who prove such connections think (and sometimes tell me) they must be entitled to special pensions or titles, or that they are themselves royal, or are actually the rightful monarch. They are wrong.

What it does mean is that you have a vast number of new ancestral lines which you can enjoy exploring. It also means, if your connection is via legitimate generations, that you have a place in the line of succession. The official list (up to no. 40) is under 'The Current Royal Family/Succession' on www.royal.gov.uk/. To calculate your place, simply draw up a family tree (based on Ruvigny's *Blood Royal*, and supplemented by your own research) of every single living person in the world who comes from a senior line to your own, count them up, and that's your number. It is almost an impossible task, of course. I had a go at making a rough estimate for myself, once: I worked out I was about 200,000th in line to the throne. But that was probably a vast under-estimate.

Chapter 14

ROYAL ROOTS ABROAD

Royal Ancestors' Ancestors

Once you have traced back to a royal ancestor, you have opened a gateway onto a realm of high genealogical adventure. In times of internal stress, royal families tended to choose their wives from (and marry their daughters to) the families of their great nobles, so as to build up alliances for themselves within their own borders.

But when monarchies were strong and confident they tended to use royal marriages as a means of creating networks of international alliances. So the King of England married the daughter of the King of France, whose mother was in turn the daughter of the King of Spain: and before you have gone very far back, you will find you have ancestors from all over Europe, and often much further afield too. Holidays abroad can become particularly interesting when you know that many of the medieval kings mentioned in the guidebooks are actually your forebears.

Many of the routes back to the distant past have been explored already. Sir Iain Moncrieffe of that Ilk's *Royal Highness: Ancestry of the Royal Child* (1982) works back from Prince William, via George VI and Queen Elizabeth the Queen Mother, and also via Lady Diana Spencer, to show William's descent from a wide range of European and Middle Eastern royal forebears. Moncrieffe's work was based on Sir Anthony Wagner's 'Bridges to Antiquity' in his *Pedigree and Progress* (1975). A recent set of genealogical tables based on these, but updated with new scholarship (especially that of Christian Settipani) and focused around the ancestry of Edward I and Edward III, has been created by Don Stone; see www.ancientdescents.com.

Many medieval marriage alliances, being key elements of royal policy, were extremely well recorded at the time, and part of the point of royal genealogies was to boast of the family's international links. However, especially going back towards AD 1000, and in the centuries before, royal lines tended to be recorded in terms of male lines only, and wives were not mentioned so often. Identifying the king's wife (and thus all of her ancestors) can be a matter for detailed scholarship: and if a king had more than one wife, which one was the mother of the child from whom you are descended?

Equally, whilst the identities of rulers are often easy to establish, the precise nature of their connections is more difficult: does a list of three kings represent grandfather, father and son, or two brothers and an uncle? Greater problems arise in looking at the early genealogy of families, such as the Carolingians in France and Germany, who had been court officials or landed magnates before attaining royal status. Here, much fascinating scholarship is needed to sort out the truth about their origins.

The piecing together of early aristocratic and royal genealogies often relies on prosopography. This is a process of fathoming out genealogical relationships based on continuity of name, place and occupation, when records exist that identify people, but which do not explicitly state their family connections. Whilst used most prominently for Dark Age royal genealogy, it is in fact a valid technique for any family tree before the time of easily available parish registers.

Prosopography's best known, most active practitioner is Christian Settipani, who has used prosopographic techniques to try to reconstruct Dark Age French genealogies, particularly those of counts whose estates, and possibly ancestry, were derived from Roman Church lands and the hereditary dynasties of clergymen who held them. A successful exercise would demonstrate that there was a hereditary principle in operation – fathers tended to pass their lands and titles down to their sons – and that a succession of similarly named people had held the same land and title: the most logical inference is that these people represent some sort of father-son chain. At best they are held together by dotted lines – the genealogists' code for 'I think they are related but I cannot quite prove it'.

The Longest Family Tree in the West

Indeed, many early royal genealogies go back to a series names, linked by dotted lines. In some cases, such dotted lines might lead back to the base of an earlier royal genealogy that is far more certain, or to a possible ancestor whose wife's family line is very well recorded.

By use of dotted lines, Wagner showed a very plausible line of descent for Edward I, via his maternal-line ancestors in medieval Byzantium, to their maternal-line royal ancestors in Armenia. Edward I's mother Eleanor of Provence was the great-granddaughter of Sanchia of

Castille and Leon, whose own mother was the Polish princess Richilda. Richilda's great-great-great-grandmother Richenza of Lorraine was the daughter of Mathilda daughter of the Byzantine Emperor Otto II (d. 983) and his wife Theophano. She was probably the daughter of the Emperor Romanus II, whose likely great-grandfather Constantine – this is the point where the dotted lines come in – was the son of Hmayeak, a prince from the Mamikonid dynasty of Dark Age Armenia.

Hmayeak, and thus, probably, Edward I (and all his descendants) was probably descended from Chosroes I, King of Armenia (d. AD 216/7), a younger son of Vologaeses IV (also sometimes numbered V), Great King of Parthia who died in AD 207/8 and ruled over much of the Middle East.

The most genealogically likely line back from this point goes via Vologaeses' wife, who was a daughter of Pharasmenes II, King of Iberia (modern Georgia, next to Armenia). His line goes back to Pharnabazus I, who died in 234 BC. He is the earliest likely ancestor we can trace for Edward I, without straying from historical plausibility.

Before then, we approach the realm of myth. The *Georgian Chronicle* (*c.* AD 500s) made Pharnabazus son of Mts'xit, whose ancestry went back (through largely unnamed generations) to T'orgom, a gigantic warrior who settled in the Caucasian mountains. T'orgom's son Hayk

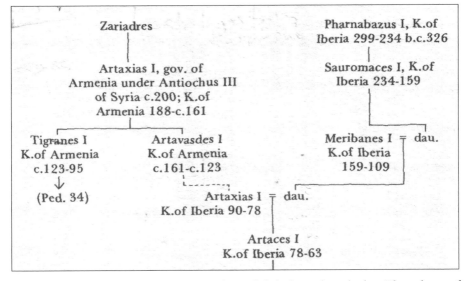

Part of the line that connects Western royalty and their descendants back to Pharnabazus of Iberia, from Wagner's Pedigree and Progress.

founded Hayastan (Armenia) and his son K'art'los founded Mts'xet, which became Iberia (Georgia). Once, we may infer, T'orgom was the god of the high-peaked mountains, but as recorded by Georgia's early Christian monks, he was said to have witnessed the destruction of the Tower of Babel, and to have been son of Tiras, son of Gomer, son of Japheth, son of Noah, who was ninth in descent from Adam and Eve.

Alexander the Great

Piecing together Vologaeses IV's paternal ancestry, from coins and inscriptions, is an uncertain exercise. So too is determining the precise origins of his dynasty's wives. They were probably descended from the Persian Great Kings, Cyrus and Darius, and through female lines (as Don Stone suggests) from the kings of Syria, and then, through the Syrian kings' wives, from the kings of Epirus. A possible ancestor, therefore, is Alexander II King of Epirus (d. 296 BC), whose mother was the sister of Alexander the Great (d. 323 BC).

The ancestry of Alexander the Great and his sister leads us into yet more glamorous territory. Their mother Olympias was daughter of Neoptolemus I, King of Epirus. He claimed descent from Neoptolemus (Pyrrhus), the son of Achilles, the hero of Homer's *Iliad*, who is said to have fought at the siege of Troy (*c.* 1194–1184 BC). Alexander's father, Philip II of Macedonia, meanwhile, came from a dynasty keen to prove itself to be Greek. To this end they had conjured up a descent from Hercules. It was a story that, having been repeated for a few generations, became widely believed throughout the classical world, and was embellished to create a plausible-looking genealogy.

Alexander the Great's descents from Hercules and Achilles had, ultimately, been worked up out of nothing. But they seemed real enough in Alexander's time. It was Alexander's personal belief in his heroic ancestry that inspired him to achieve what nobody could have imagined possible – the conquest of most of the known world.

Such splendid links back from Edward I to Pharnabazus, and to the sister of Alexander, involve varying degrees of speculation: it would be wonderful if they were definitely true, but we are a long way off proving them. Each 'probable/possible' link involves a degree of uncertainty, which cumulatively add up to considerable doubt.

On the other hand, kings *did* seek out wives from older dynasties – often deliberately making marriage alliances between their heirs and the older lines they had supplanted, so as to arrogate to their own line the inherited authority of the past. On that basis, it is likely enough that the Armenian kings had the blood of Alexander's family in their veins: the routes Stone and others have mapped out are simply the most likely ones that we can find.

The works above, by Wagner, Moncrieffe and Stone, incorporate much of this scholarship. Their writings on the subject are all worth reading. New developments are added to Stone's charts and are chronicled by M.L. Bierbrier in his 'New Developments in Medieval Genealogy' column in the *Genealogist's Magazine*, the journal of the Society of Genealogists.

Alexander the Great (356–323 BC), commemorated at his birthplace, Pella, Macedonia.

Much of this has made its way onto the Internet, but with a considerable amount of irresponsible or unfounded speculation thrown in. Sites such as www.fabpedigree.com/ contain much genuine material, and much (self-confessedly) wild speculation, without distinguishing between the two – so render themselves far less useful than they would be otherwise.

Sources for Foreign Aristocracy and Royalty

Sources for non-British nobility include Ruvigny's *Titled Nobility of Europe: an international peerage or 'Who's Who' of the Sovereigns, Princes and Nobles of Europe* (1914), which includes truncated genealogies. The 1963 edition of *Burke's Peerage* has a section on the foreign descendants of the Stuarts, Hanovers and Saxe-Coburgs and also a revised Mountbatten pedigree.

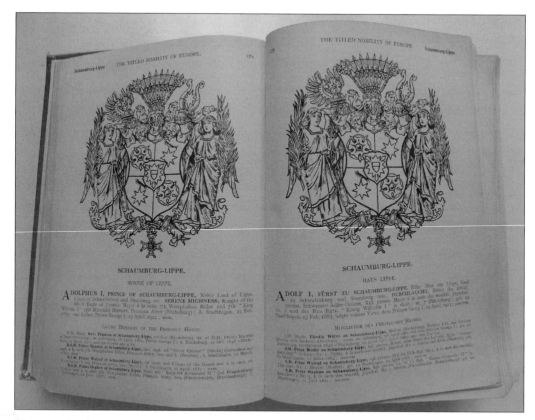

The entry for the Princes of Schaumburg-Lippe in Ruvigny's bi-lingual Titled Nobility of Europe.

The 'Burke's Peerage' of European titles is the *Almanach de Gotha*, which appeared in many editions and has a useful genealogical content. Also helpful is Baron Freytag von Loringhoven's revision of Prince Isenburg's *Stammtafeln zur Geschichte der Europaischen Staaten* (1980–95); Aubert de la Chesnaye-Des Bois' *Dictionaire de la Noblesse* (3rd edn 1863–76), mainly concerned with France; *Elenco de Grandezas Titulos Nobiliarios Espanoles* (for Spain); W. Wegener's *Genealogische Tafeln zur mitteleuropaischen Geschichte* (1962–9); *Genealogisches Handbuch des Adels*; the *Genealogisches Handbuch des Adels*; and the *Adels-Lexiconister*.

Most useful of all for genealogical purposes is A.M.H.J. Stokvis' *Manuel d'Histoire, de Genealogie et de Chronologie de tous les etats du*

Swiatopolk - Mirski

Orthodoxes et catholiques. – Titre princier reconnu par la députation du Sénat du Royaume de Pologne 27 mai 1821 et en Russie par oukaze impérial du 18 avril 1861 (pour Thomas-Bogumił-Jean Swiatopolk-Mirski et ses fils avec leur postérité). Confirmation du titre princier par arrêts du Sénat Dirigeant du 24 nov. 1881 et 20 janv. 1886. – Armes: v. l'édition de 1924, p. 473. – Les cadets portent le nom de prince ou princesse de Swiatopolk-Mirski.

Dimitri kniaz (prince) Swiatopolk-Mirski, né à Hievka 27 août 1890, fils du pr. Pierre, né 18 août 1857, † 16 mai 1914, et de Catherine née ctesse Bobrinsky, née 24 sept. 1864, m. 19 janv. 1886, † 22 avril 1926; prof. de litérature russe à l'univ. de Londres, ancien capit. de la garde russe. [*Londres W 1, 17 Gower Street.*]

Sœurs

1. Psse *Sophie*, née à Kouskovo 30 mai 1887, ancienne demoiselle d'honn. des feues impératrices de Russie; m. à Athènes 27 avril 1923 à Serge Pakhitonoff, ing., ancien lt. du génie russe. [*Grenoble, Isère, 18 Chemin des Buttes.*]
2. Psse *Olga*, née à Jécaterinoslav 18 févr. 1899. [*Paris IX, 4 rue de Turin.*]

Frère du grand-père

du mariage du bisaïeul le pr. Thomas-Bogumił-Jean (v. ci-dessus), né 15 déc. 1788, † . . . . 1868, avec Marcienne Nostitz-Jackowska, née . . . . 1807, m. . . . . 1822, † 27 oct. 1853.

† Pr. Nicolas, né à Miastków 5 juill. 1833, † à Mir 15 juill. 1898, ataman des cosaques du Don, gén. de cav. russe et aide de camp gén., mbre du Conseil de l'Empire; m.: 1° à Tiflis . . . . 1860 à Véra psse de Géorgie, née à Tiflis . . . . 1842, † à Vladikavkaz . . . . 1861; 2° à St. Pétersbourg 14 avril 1868 à Cléopatre Khanykoff, née à St-Pétersbourg 5 déc. 1845, † à Mir 18 févr. 1910.

Fils du 2d lit: 1) Pr. *Michel*, né à Tsarskoïe-Selo 17 juill. 1870, chambellan et ancien chargé d'affaires russe à Sophia. [*Chât. de Mir, Pologne.*]

Part of a typical entry from the Almanach de Gotha.

Princess Maria Sviatopolk-Mirski, whose family fled the Russian Revolution. Maria grew up in great hardship in Germany and London, and she only found out she was a princess when she was 9. She has been exploring her aristocratic ancestry ever since.

Part of the genealogy of the Princes of Schaumburg-Lippe, from Stokvis' Manuel.

Globe (1888–93, repr. 1966) and partly online at http://tinyurl.com/ctduhry. Useful for trying to go further back are the detailed genealogical tables in David R. Sear's *The Emperors of Rome and Byzantium* (1974).

An excellent bibliography of European nobility is Frederick R. Pryce's *A guide to European genealogies exclusive of the British Isles: with an historical survey of the principal genealogical writers* (typescript thesis, 1965), a copy of which is at the Society of Genealogists.

Both the Society of Genealogists and Institute of Heraldic and Genealogical Studies have fine collections of relevant material.

Dracula

The royal ancestry of royalty is a periodic source of excitement for the press. In 1998 the *Sun* printed this perfectly silly, yet factually accurate piece 'revealing' that Prince Charles was descended from Count Dracula, and included a pedigree back from his great-grandmother Mary of Teck, through her father's mother's Hungarian ancestors, to the bloodthirsty Vlad IV, Voivode of Transylvania (d. 1507), who was awarded the Order of the Dragon, so was nicknamed 'Dragl'. I am sure Prince Charles was as amused as everyone else at the accompanying picture, which showed him replete with slicked-back hair and a pair of fangs emerging from his upper jaw.

Links Across the World

Genealogical connections between rulers do not stop with the Middle East. In *Pedigree and Progress*, Wagner shows an indirect link between Henry III of England (d. 1272) and his contemporary Kublai Khan, Emperor of China (d. 1294), grandson of Ghengis Khan (Kublai's nephew Abaka, Ilkhan of Persia, married Maria, a natural daughter of Michael VIII Palaeologus, Emperor of Byzantium, whose son Emperor Andronicus II married Anna of Hungary, whose sister Maria married Charles II of Naples, whose mother Beatrix was sister of Eleanor of Provence, wife of Henry III of England).

These are not just interesting connections for their son Edward I's descendants. They also have a far great resonance for all our un-traceable, non-royal medieval genealogical lines, for they are good indicators of the wider movements of people. For every ruler's wife or child who moved between countries, so too did countless diplomats, servants, merchants and armies. One royal genealogical link between two countries therefore indicates the hidden presence of many more such potential genealogical connections at lower social levels. The interconnected network of royal families that spans the past couple of thousand years is therefore a sort of map, indicating much greater movements of human genes that are likely to have taken place, and that affect us all.

The bloodlines leading down to Edward I are common to vast numbers of British families and their colonial descendants. But you may find other links to foreign aristocrats and royalty by less trodden routes. Sir Winston Churchill and many others are descended from the marriage of Thomas Darcy (d. 1593) and Camilla Guicciarddini, whose grandmother Camilla Bardi was a sixth cousin of Lorenzo 'the Magnificent' de Medici (d. 1492), ruler of Florence.

Elizabeth Woodville, wife of Edward IV, had a sister Agnes, who married William Dormer of West Wycombe, Buckinghamshire, whose blood flows in many local aristocratic, gentry and, ultimately, ordinary family lines (and, via the Havers family, to me). The Woodville girls' mother Jacquetta was daughter of Margueritte, Countess of Saint-Pol, whose own mother Sueva de Baux, Duchess of Andrea, was daughter of Nicolo Orsini (d. 1399), Count of Nola. He was a member of the medieval Roman senate, with impeccable Roman ancestry, and he was also great-great-great-great-grandfather of Pope Paul III (Alessandro Farnese). Paul III's sister Giulia Farnese was lover of Pope Alexander VI and mother of his illegitimate child, Giovani Borgia (d. 1548), Duke of Camerina. Such aristocratic connections were probably not dreamed of by their distant cousins in the Buckinghamshire countryside.

Huguenot ancestry can be another route back to aristocracy. Huguenots were French Protestant refugees who settled (mainly) in England and Ireland in the seventeenth century, especially after the Revocation of the Edict of Nantes in 1685. Refugees came from all classes, but with a bias towards those merchants and aristocrats who could afford to escape. The published transactions of the Huguenot Society (http://tinyurl.com/bv4tjam) are often all you will need to trace back, though please remember that not all families with French surnames (or French-sounding surnames) were Huguenots, for many other French people migrated here at other times, and for other reasons.

Burke's Royal Families of the World: Africa and the Middle East (1980) can be just the start of your adventures in taking connections further, outside Europe. Many black British families know their descent from African tribal kings, and a vast number more must have such descents, but not know it.

All Hindus of Brahmin and Ksatriya castes derive their genealogy and caste membership, ultimately, from the extended, semi-mythical genealogy of Manu Vivasvata ('the man born of the sun'), said to have lived *c.* 2,000–3,000 BC. They have genealogies (many of which are kept for them by the priests at Varanasi) tracing at least some way back towards one of Manu's named descendants.

Many Han Chinese have descents, recorded in *jiapus* or family genealogy books, from the mythical Emperor Huangdi, 'the Yellow Emperor' (d. 2597 BC).

The claims of Gentiles to have Biblical descent, through lines going down from the family of Jesus into Dark Age French nobility, and to the family of the British king Caratacus, are fables, based on Dark Age and medieval longings, laudable in their own contexts, to connect royal pedigrees back to Adam and Eve, a subject to which we will return in the last chapter.

Many Jewish families must be descended from the House of David (see http://davidicdynasty.net/). The Dayyanshare have an unbroken pedigree and several others such as the Shaltiels, Charlaps and Serriors have good claims to Davidic descent. However, Zuckerman's theory that one line converted to Christianity and became Dukes of Acquitaine has been roundly disproved.

Plenty of British and American Jews belong to the Cohenim and Levite castes, the priests and assistants, respectively, in the synagogues, and have surnames reflecting this: Cohenim surnames can include Carr, Kahn, Kagan, Kaplinsk and so on. All true Levites are said to descend in the male line from Levi, son of Jacob and Leah, whilst the Cohenim are a sub-set of the Levites, established by Zadok the Priest, and restricted to the male-line progeny of Levi's great-grandson Aaron, the brother of Moses.

Because these groups claimed male-line continuity over some 3,300 years, they were ideal subjects for early male-line, Y chromosome tests, pioneered at www.familytreedna.com. It turned out that about half those claiming to be Cohenim did not match up: over the violent and disrupted history of Jewry, much had gone awry. But the extraordinary result of the tests was that, from the wealthy Sephardim of Western Europe to the impoverished Ashkenazim of Eastern Europe and even the black Jews of Africa, just under half of those claiming to be Cohenim *did* match up – and thus proving genuine continuity, and the truth of their passionately held traditions. The tests are easily available, and if they prove positive for you, then you will be able to prove that you have some extremely distinguished Jewish aristocratic ancestry indeed.

A Right Royal Surprise

Sometimes, royal ancestors are beyond any sort of prediction. Retired headteacher Jacquie Buttriss traced back her Jewish family tree to a rabbi, Aron Teomim Frankel (1630–90), whose mother was Beila Wahl Katzenellenbogen. Her father Meir was son of Saul Katzenellenbogen (1545–1617), who had become a friend and favourite counsellor to Prince Radziwill. In 1587, King Stefan Bathori of Poland died and the Polish nobles convened to elect a new king. The law dictated that the new king must be elected within a day, but as the hour-glass sand trickled away, they realised they needed more time. At Prince Radziwill's suggestion, they elected a trusted, neutral figure, to be king for 24 hours, to give them long enough to make their final choice. And thus Jacquie Buttriss's ancestor Saul Katzenellenbogen became, for one day, the King of Poland.

Chapter 15

CLANS AND KINGS OF SCOTLAND AND IRELAND

The Clans of Scotland and Ireland

If you have Scots or Irish ancestry, you have even better reason than most to investigate the origins of your surname, using the books identified in the chapter on surnames. All 'Mac' and 'O' surnames commemorate the name of the family's founder. MacDonald is 'son of Donald', O'Connor is 'descendant of Connor'. The origins of some of these eponymous founders is unknown, but in many cases they come complete with a pedigree, that will often go back to Scots or Irish royalty.

Such pedigrees may seem entirely fabulous, but they stand up to considerable scrutiny. The clan system was the product of a fiercely Iron Age society in which the king and his *derbfine*, his close male-line kin, held absolute power. When the king appointed a chieftain to a region, it was bound to be one of his male-line kin, and when that man in turn tenanted his land, he would favour his own sons and immediate male-line relations. All the advantages lay with the *derbfine*, so it would dominate a wide area rapidly, and the clans and septs that sprung up afterwards would, more likely than not, be of that same powerful male-line strain.

There were surely cases of families claiming illustrious connections where none really existed, and of kings tacitly agreeing to the lie in order to secure the alliance of the clan concerned. However, when geneticists started testing the male-line DNA signatures of clans who claimed to have the same male-line ancestry, they were surprised to find that, more often than not, the relevant genes really did match up.

The genealogies of clan chiefs were recited frequently and proudly by their hereditary bards, at feasts and funerals, and every time their armies goaded themselves for battle. Later, they were recorded, by monks and scribes, and are all in print.

The Anglo-Norman families who settled in Ireland, and those whom the Scots kings encouraged to settle in Scotland, rapidly started behaving like clans too, favouring their own *derbfine* of sons and grandsons over other tenants. They quickly populated the lands they had been granted with their own kin, so before long the Sinclairs' lands were full of Sinclairs, the Frasers' with Frasers, and so on.

An earlier wave of immigrants, the Vikings, who sailed round via the Orkneys and Shetland Islands and colonised parts of western Scotland, the Isle of Man and Dublin and Waterford in Ireland, also adopted the clan system. Western Isles clans like the MacLeods of Harris, Lewis and Assynt, Clan Gunn and many of the Nicholsons and Mathesons are of Norse (and in some cases royal Norse) roots.

J. Logan's *The Clans of the Scottish Highlands* (1845) and Roddy Martine's *Scottish Clans and Family Names* (1987, new edn 1996) are two of a host of books providing potted summaries of Scots clans and their origins. The main Scottish clan genealogies are in the 107th edition of *Burke's Peerage*. There are privately printed books on the histories and genealogies of most clans, which will often go into detail over junior branches. The shelves and online catalogue of the Society of Genealogists (www.sog.org.uk) and the National Library of Scotland (www.nls.uk/catalogues) are good places to start looking.

The ruins of Ardvreck Castle on Loch Assynt, Sutherland, former seat of the warlike McLeods of Assynt, a Scottish sept of Viking origin.

Most clans have societies, which advertise in the *Highlander* magazine (www.highlandermagazine.com) and most now have websites. The Electric Scotland website at http://tinyurl.com/d6vjcrz is a good portal for finding these. My book *Tracing Your Scottish Family History* (2008) includes two pedigrees showing the descent of many of the clans with royal Scots and Viking roots.

Linked to the clan societies are DNA projects for many Scots and Irish clan surnames. Most are on www.familytreedna.com/projects.aspx.

Connecting Back to Clans

Clan membership is a vexed and often misunderstood matter. Maps sold to tourists in Scotland and Ireland show the locations of clan names, whilst gift shops selling mugs, keyrings and tartans encourage you to believe that if your surname is one of those shown, you must belong to the clan. That is nonsense, because many surnames have multiple origins. Some Nicholsons, for example, come from Clan Nicolson in Aberdeen, descended from Nicholas, son of Gille Muire, descended from Harald the Viking. But other Nicholsons are from a Gaelic family, MacNicol or MacNeacail of Scorrybreac in Skye and yet others still are from Lowland Scots or English families who happened to have an ancestor called Nicholas or Nichol, who had nothing to do with clans at all.

If you can trace your ancestry back to a Nicolson from Aberdeen or a MacNichol from Skye, then you are on much firmer ground for claiming membership of one of those two clans. Some purists would still carp, saying that sometimes people living on clan lands would change their surname to that of the clan, so as to gain that clan's protection. Doubtless, this happened occasionally, but it cannot have been a widespread practice: the point of clans was to keep outsiders out, and clan genealogies were remembered meticulously, so a simple change of name was never going to fool anybody. A Nicholson in Skye may have been a Campbell in Nicholson's clothing – but it was far more likely that he was, simply, a genuine Nicholson of Skye!

If you are lucky, sufficient records will survive to enable you to trace back and link yourself to an established clan genealogy, and show how your crofting family were younger sons of small farmers, who were the younger sons of tacksmen (larger, lease-holding farmers), who came from a junior branch of the clan's family. If so, you will prove yourself kin to the current chief.

The Scots kings tried to tame the clans by converting clan chiefs into titled aristocrats, who were re-granted their own tribal lands by royal charter. So you could very well find that the head of your family is in fact, for example, the Earl of Erroll (if you are a Hay) or the Duke of Argyll (if you are a Campbell).

In many cases, Irish and Scottish records are sadly not up to the job of tracing so far back. More likely than not, you will end up with your line topped by a question mark. Whilst you will be reasonably sure you are descended from the earlier clan chiefs, you won't have a hope of proving exactly how. However, you can use DNA testing to strengthen your case. A male-line, Y chromosome test on yourself (or a male relative of yours who bears the relevant surname) can be compared with the genetic profiles of definite descendants of the clan in question (perhaps even the chief himself). A match will confirm that your family is from the same stock as theirs. Such a DNA test will not tell you from which of a long line of chiefs your own branch split off, but you will know that the founder, at least, must have been your ancestor. In such cases, a dotted line back from your earliest proven ancestor to the founder of the clan is a perfectly acceptable and sensible thing to put on a family tree.

A Campbell Coincidence

One day the National Maritime Museum invited me to join in their East India family history day, speaking to and giving advice to visitors. But what they told me was far more interesting than anything I could tell them. One lady told me how she had traced her Campbell family tree back, via a generation or two living in Calcutta as employees of the East India Company, to a line of Scots Campbells who she had traced back to the family of the Duke of Argyll. When she went to visit Inveraray Castle, she introduced herself to the duke as one of his many long-lost cousins and she said 'he gave me a lovely big hug'. Later the same day, I spoke to an elderly Indian gentleman who had traced his family tree back to a mixed race union between an Indian lady and an early nineteenth-century British lawyer called Donald Campbell, who had gone out to practise in India. He was not directly connected to the East India Company Campbells, above, but as a trained lawyer he was obviously from a moneyed background, so could very well have belonged to another junior line of the Duke of Argyll's family.

Scots Royalty

On the death of Elizabeth I in 1603, James VI Stuart, King of Scots became James I of England. This was because his great-grandmother, the wife of James IV, was the daughter of Henry VII of England. The Stuarts had become kings of Scots through the marriage of Robert II Stuart to Marjory, daughter of Robert the Bruce (d. 1329), King of Scots. They gained their surname because, before they were kings, they had been Great Stewards of Scotland. Their ancestry goes back to an immigrant, Walter Fitz Alan (d. 1177), who was in turn descended from Alan, seneschal or steward to the Counts of Dol in Brittany, to whom he was probably related.

Robert the Bruce had inherited the Scots throne through the marriage of his own great-grandfather Robert Bruce, Lord of Annandale with Isabella, daughter of David, Earl of Huntingdon, a younger brother of William the Lion (d. 1214), King of Scots. William and David were grandsons of King David (d. 1153), son of Malcolm III Canmore, King of Scots. Malcolm's daughter Matilda had married Henry I of England, providing Henry and all his English descendants with a healthy dose of royal Scots blood.

Malcolm and his immediate successors inherited a country that had altered little since the Iron Age. Learning many lessons from the Normans – Malcolm's son David spent forty years at the English court before succeeding to his father's throne – they introduced

The Moot Hill at Scone, near Perth, the traditional place of enthronement of the Kings of Scots, and long-time home of the Stone of Scone.

155

feudalism into Lowland Scotland. They deliberately granted much of the Lowlands to Norman and Breton knights, hoping thus to civilise their unruly people. The Bruce family was one of many families of incomers: their ancestor was Robert de Bruis, of Norman origin, to whom David granted the Lairdship of Annandale in 1124. Many other families, who we think of now as being innately Scottish, arrived around this time too – Frasers, Gordons, Hamiltons, Sinclairs, Boyles and so on, each with a clearly identified aristocratic ancestor, from whom a goodly number of those who now bear their names are descended.

The Scots kings also sought to make feudal subjects of the savagely independent chieftains of the Highlands and the *mormaers*, lords of ancient origin who held territorial authority over wider swathes of the rugged landscape. Slowly, the mormaers were brought under royal control by being regranted to their holders as earldoms. Many lines ended (conveniently) with heiresses who were married to royal princes or Lowland (Anglo-Norman) barons, thus bringing their blood down to modern times.

Malcolm III's father King Duncan – he who was murdered by MacBeth – was himself the son of Crinan, Mormaer of Athole, who married Bethan, daughter of King Malcolm II (d. 1034). Bethan's sister and (arguably) co-heiress was MacBeth's mother Donada. Crinan's family were also hereditary abbots (or *co arbs*) of Dunkeld, where they guarded the relics of St Columba. It has been inferred, and widely accepted, that Crinan's family were part of the Cineal Conaill, the kindred of the descendants of St Columbas' family – and Columba was son of Conall Gulban, a son of Niall of the Nine Hostages, High King of Ireland *c.* AD 450.

What makes Crinan's line even more interesting is that it produced a number of prolific younger branches. From Malcolm III's younger son Malcolm descend the Robertsons, and hence the Skenes, whilst Duncan's younger son Maldred, who became Earl of Northumberland, produced a number of male-line descendants, whose surnames were derived from their estates, or from heiresses they married. Robert, a great-great-great-grandson of Maldred, married the heiress of the Nevilles, and produced the later Neville Earls of Westmorland and Warwick, including the famous 'Kingmaker', whilst William, a great-great-great-great-grandson of Maldred, was lord of Washington, County Durham, and was ancestor of George Washington, President of the United States. All, we may infer, were descendants, via the

Columba depicted in stained glass at Dunkeld Cathedral, Scotland. Sprung from the High Kings of Ireland, he was an ancestor of the later kings of Scotland, and many English families including the Washingtons.

Scots kings and the family of St Columba, of Niall of the Nine Hostages. How's that for aristocratic ancestry?

Malcolm II of Scots, whose daughter Bethan conveyed the throne into Crinan's family, was a great-great-grandson of Kenneth McAlpin (d. 859). Families descended from Kenneth's junior progeny include the MacKinnons, MacQuarries, Gregors of Golden Bridles, MacGregors, Grants, MacFees, Griersons and Griers.

Kenneth's parents were Alpin, King of Dalriada, and a Pictish princess, probably a daughter of King Constantine I of the Picts (d. 820).

157

King Malcolm Ceann-mor, killed 1093

King David the Saint, died 1153

Henry, Earl of Northumberland, died c.1152

David, Earl of Huntingdon, died 1219

Lady Isabel the Scot married

Robert Bruce, Lord of Annan

Robert Bruce, tanist of

Robert Bruce, Ea

King Rob

Pri

PROOF

Part of the pedigree of the Scots kings, from Iain Moncreiffe's Blood Royal *(1956), brilliantly illustrated by Don Pottinger.*

Dalriada was a kingdom in western Scotland, centred on Dunadd in Argyll. It had been founded by Alpin's 8 × great-grandfather, Fergus Mor Mac Erca (d. AD 501). The Dalriadans were 'Scots', a term that meant, originally, 'Gaels from Ireland' and which only later became a term for anyone living in northern Britain. Dalriada and Pictland had long been at war, but with Kenneth there began the process of welding them into a single realm, called at first 'Alba' (from the ancient name for Britain, Albion, 'the white island') and (much later) 'Scotland'.

Fergus Mor Mac Erca, founder of Dalriada and ancestor of the early Scots kings, was of Irish stock: he was said to have been a younger son of Muireadach, son of Eoghan, a younger son of Niall of the Nine Hostages himself.

Over the ensuing centuries, the Dalriadan dynasty expanded its territories across all of what we now call Scotland and founded many Scottish family lines. From Fergus' brother Lorne, Lord of Lorne, descended the MacLeans, the MacNabs, the mormaers of Moray (including MacBeth), the Murrays, MacKays and MacWilliams.

Myself at Dunadd, Argyll. The ancient kings of Dalriada were inaugurated here, by standing in the footprint carved into the rock (below my right wellington).

Fergus' brother Oengus was ancestor of the MacInneses. Their elder brother Muirceartach remained in Ireland: amongst his descendants who came later were the Buchanans, Munros, Macmillans, MacNeills of Barra, MacLachlans, Lamonts, MacSorleys, the MacSweenys (alias MacQueens) and the MacEwans of Otter.

Picts and their Queens

The Dalriadan Scots expanded at the expense of the Picts. 'Pict' was the name the Romans had given the native peoples of northern Britain. Their own name for themselves was probably *Pit*, a name that survives in many north-east Scottish place names: calling them 'Picts', 'the painted ones', was probably a Roman pun, for the Picts painted their bodies with blue woad.

Pictish society was so ancient that it had not yet made the transition to male-line succession from the older practice of inheriting power through the female line. They seem still to have worshipped the Great Mother, whom they called Bride or Bruide or Brigid, who later became the Christian St Brigid. They had kings to lead their armies, but the king's authority rested on his being married – presumably by common consent – to the queen, and the succession passed down to the eldest daughter, whose husband would be the next king: in each generation, the queen was seen not so much as an entity in her own right, as a reincarnation of her ancestress, the goddess Bride herself.

The Picts' royal pedigree was recorded in the *Pictish King List*, a transcript of which appears in William F. Skene's *Chronicles of the Picts, Chronicles of the Scots and other Early Memorials of Scottish History* (1867) (available at http://books.google.co.uk/). A copy of the list is at http://tinyurl.com/blvs2rp. It is reasonably accurate back to the AD 400s: it purports to go back to about 1,000 BC, and for all we know it could be accurate, except for the earliest couple of generations before King Gede Olgudach. These, in the version we have now, have clearly been manipulated by Irish monks, influenced by Greek tradition. Instead of the goddess Bride as the ultimate ancestress of the line, we have Cruithne, whose name is an Irish eponym for 'Britain', and his sons, all of whose names are eponyms for parts of Scotland.

The Gaels of Dalriada were keen to subvert history by pretending they had been in Scotland longer than the Picts, so they picked up on a phrase in Virgil's *Aeneid*, 'picti Agathyrsi', the 'painted Agathirsi' of Thrace, and invented a story that the Picts had come in ships from Russia (and ultimately from Thrace). The Greeks had given the Agathirsi an eponymous ancestor, Agathyrsus, born after an encounter between Echidna and Hercules, so the Gaelic monks gave Cruithne a pedigree going back to 'Ercol', the Gaelic for Hercules.

It is possible to find family lines that may go back to this extraordinary pedigree. One version of the Duffs' ancestry deduces them from Connall Cerr, son of the Pictish king Eochaid Bruide. MacNaughton means 'son of Nechtan', a name (albeit Gaelic in origin) used by several Pictish kings, and possibly denoting descent from one of them. However, the strongest line of descent from the Pictish kings comes through the marriage of Alpin, King of the Dalriadan Scots, with his royal Pictish wife. All the medieval Scots and English kings were descended from them, so all had a small dose of royal (and, ultimately, divine) Pictish blood in their veins.

Celtic Roots

The population of north-west Europe comes from the Mesolithic descendants of the hunter-gatherer bands who spread north from the rocky refuges of southern France and northern Spain at the end of the last Ice Age, mixed with descendants of Neolithic farmers, who spread up subsequently from the eastern Mediterranean.

In the centuries before the Roman invasions of Gaul and Britain, the farming tribes of northern Europe experienced three technological convulsions, both triggered by contact with the Mediterranean world. In central Europe, from the 700s BC, under 'Hallstatt Culture', the efficiency of newly developed iron weapons engendered a thoroughly unpleasant society, dominated by young, violent warriors whose faith in the druidic concept of reincarnation made them wrecklessly fearless in battle.

Contact with the classical world stimulated the more sophisticated 'La Tène Culture', from about 450 BC, characterised by the use of two-wheeled chariots, a method of warfare imported, ultimately, from Mesopotamia. Spreading rapidly outwards, these warriors, and those who adopted the same behaviour, are termed Gauls, Galatians, Gallicians, Gaels or, generally, 'Celts'.

Iron-working entered Britain about 400 BC, probably through invasion. The Victorian notion of the entire population of Britain and Ireland being replaced wholesale by Celts has long been disproved, but it is likely that the tribes of southern Britain and southern Ireland, as they existed in Caesar's time, had a substantial La Tène, 'Celtic' element.

Meanwhile, in north-east France and Belgium, the mixture of La Tène Celts with Germanic peoples bred the hybrid warrior race known to Caesar as the Belgae. Some Belgic tribes, particularly the Catuvellauni and Atrebates, made violent incursions into south-east Britain, whilst those remembered as the 'Fir Bolg' appeared in south-east Ireland as well.

Wherever they settled, the Celts overlaid the older mixed Mesolithic and Neolithic population, to whom they were of course related. Many native male lineages were extinguished, or nearly so, and the male lines of the Celtic warlords proliferated aggressively. Before long these Celts, called Gaels or *Scots*, had taken over most of Ireland. Most royal dynasties across Ireland claimed to be of Gaelic stock, as did the kings of Dalriada in what became Scotland. Modern genetics suggests that most of them were telling the truth.

Irish Genealogies

Most Irish royal and tribal genealogies are considered to be reliable back to about the AD 300s, a handful of generations before Christianity arrived and monks started writing down oral traditions. The links claimed by the pedigrees often stand up to robust genetic testing. Some of the lines may be accurate further back too. But when they extend back to Heber, Heremon and Ir, the sons of Milesius, King of Spain, and their kin, *c.* 1700 BC, as recorded in the *Lebor Gabála Érenn* (*The Book of the Conquest of Ireland*), we know we have entered the realm of myth.

Once Christianity arrived in the AD 400s, monks started recording the oral pedigrees of the kings and chiefs. Most seem to have stretched back, as one would expect, ten or twenty generations, and started with a god. For example, the Eóganacht kings of Munster in southern Ireland claimed descent from a god called Eógan Már. Niall of the Nine Hostages's ancestors, the Connachta of the west, who spread out to dominate Ulster, claimed descent from Conn Cétchathach, god of battles.

Tribal alliances were probably sealed or dissolved on the basis of the interrelationships and wars of such deities, but the monks who recorded Irish traditions made a point of euhemerising the old gods, claiming they had simply been powerful men. The monks gave them made-up pedigrees of human ancestors, and replaced the gods' unifying roles by making these lineages link up. Ultimately, the monks derived most lines of the northern and western dynasties from Heremon, and most of the southern ones from Heber, two mythical heroes, said the monks, who had led a mythical Gaelic conquest of Ireland – a conquest that roughly echoed the real (but much later) invasion by the Belgae. In time, other members of the same family were added, such as Heber and Heremon's brother Ir, and their uncle Ithe, from whom various Irish clans claimed descent.

The real Gaels had come to Ireland from northern Europe. In the myth, they embarked from Brigantia, in Gallicia in north-west Spain. The spot was not chosen randomly: this was where Hercules had founded the port-city of Corunna. It seems likely that, in the late Iron Age or the early Roman period, the Gaels had developed a myth deducing their origins from the progeny of Hercules. Later, the wanderings of Aeneas, as told in Virgil's *Aeneid*, suggested a more appealing possibility. One re-imaging of the story appears in the *Life of St Cadroe* (*c.* AD 900s). What seems to have happened is that, earlier, another version of this story was merged with that of Hercules: Hercules was forgotten, and the descendants attributed to him were grafted onto the family of Aeneas instead. It was all pure myth, but through such stories the pagan Irish had sought to connect themselves to the glittering culture of the Mediterranean.

In time, Aeneas morphed into a Gaelic hero, Feinius Farsaid, ancestor of the Milesian founders of Ireland. The full story in its finished form was recounted in the *Lebor Gabála Érenn* (*The Book of the Conquest of Ireland*), written about AD 1000. The Christian monks who composed this had forgotten or glossed over Hercules and Aeneas, but retained the idea of a pedigree connecting Heremon and Heber back to the eastern Mediterranean. For them this served a new and important goal: to provide a genealogical bridge for the Irish back to that golden lure of all Christian genealogy – the family of Noah. And thus, according to the *Lebor Gabála*, all Irish dynasties descend, via the Milesian family of Heremon and Heber, from Noah, and thus from Adam and Eve themselves.

The Surname Crowley

Crowley has two origins: many are from places called Crawley in England, but the Irish Crowleys' surname is an Anglicisation of O Chruadhlaoich, 'descendant of Chruadhlaoich', a Gaelic personal name meaning 'hard warrior'. Most people with Irish Crowley roots will trace them back to Co. Cork, but the sept only migrated there (as galloglasses, or hired mercenaries) in the 1280s. They came from Roscommon, and some Crowleys still remain there, and over the border in Leitrim.

The sept was descended from Chruadhlaoich, of course. He himself was a MacDermot, descended from Dermot, King of Moylurg (d. 1159), and Dermot was an O Mulrooney, named after his ancestor Maelruanadha Mor, who fought at the Battle of Clontarf in 1014, and was nicknamed 'hard warrior' by the High King, Brian Boru. Maelruanadha was a younger son of Tadgh of the Three Towers, King of Connaught (d. 956), whose ancestry can be traced back to Eochu Mugmedón, brother of High King Niall of the Nine Hostages. He in turn descended from Conn of the Hundred Battles, a euhemerised battle-god, whom the *Lebor Gabála Érenn* made into a descendant of Heremon, son of Mil, descendant of Noah.

The Crowleys of Glasgow, whose ancestors fled the 1840s Potato Famine when it struck their home at Annaduff, Co. Leitrim, where they had lived in close proximity to their ancestral homeland just over the border in Co. Roscommon.

Irish Sources

Edward MacLysaght's *Irish Families: their names, arms & origins* (1957) and the 1982 edition of his *More Irish Families* (which incorporates his *Supplement to Irish Families*) provide a balanced account of the alleged genealogical origins of the main Irish septs and clans.

The ancient, oral Irish pedigrees, as recorded and manipulated into the Milesian system, exist in several major collections. M.A. O'Brien's *Corpus Genealogiarum Hiberniae* (1962) endeavoured to collect the best of these together, naming some 13,000 people alive before the twelfth century: it includes the *Book of Leinster Genealogies*, the *Great Book of Lecan* and *The Book of Ballymote*. Useful too is T. O'Raithbheartaig's

Genealogical Tracts 1: A. The Introduction to the Book of Genealogies; B. The Ancient Tract on the Distribution of the Aithechthuatha; C. The Lecan Miscellany (1932).

A more readable, if somewhat less scholarly source, is John O'Hart's *Irish Pedigrees* (1892, repr. 1999). The first volume catalogues Gaelic families, and the second concerns incoming families from England and Wales. O'Hart's laudable aim was to show that the 'mere Irishe' had a considerably more noble history than their English oppressors, and that their lines all went back, ultimately, to Noah. He was also an avid scholar of his own aristocratic ancestry, for considerable prominence is given in his monumental work to his own family of O'Hart who were, he proclaimed proudly, the Princes of Tara and Chiefs of Sligo. Many of his pedigrees all link back, satisfyingly, and as their monkish compilers had intended, to the main stems of Heber, Heremon and their kin.

In addition, the Society of Genealogists has 'Ancient Irish pedigrees, from Japhet Mac Noah to AD. 1265' (anon. Mss, 1908). My book *Tracing Your Irish Family History* (2007) includes a pedigree of the main descendants of Heber and Heremon (and lists of some of the many families descended from them), and a more focused one of the Uí Néills of Ulster and the families they spawned. It also has a pedigree showing the intermarriage of the Norman Barry family with the Irish kings and the dissemination of their mixed blood into the Morriseys, Raymonds, Carews, Welches, FitzGeralds, FitzGibbons, Wogans, Barrymores, MacAdams, Fitz Stephens, Steynes and the Earls of March (and thence into the later Plantagenets).

As with Scotland, there are countless specialist publications, societies and DNA projects for Ireland's families, septs and clans. The National Library of Ireland's catalogue, http://www.nli.ie/en/intro/catalogues-and-databases-introduction.aspx, is a good place to start for books See also www.celts.org/clans/ for societies and www.familytree dna.com for surname-related genetic projects.

Irish Lines on the Mainland

Many Irish lines, aristocratic or not, were founded by Scots, Welsh and Anglo-Norman families settling there over the centuries, due particularly to the first English invasion in the twelfth century, and the Plantations (of Protestant settlers on land confiscated from Catholics) in the sixteenth and seventeenth centuries.

There was a trade-off in the other direction, too. The Kings of Dyfed, Wales claimed descent from Aed Brosc, an Irish warlord from Meath who claimed descent from Fiacha Suidhne of the Connachta dynasty (descended from Heremon). Another descendant of Fiacha, Daidmuid ua Duibhne, is said to have settled in Argyll where he was ancestor of the Campbells.

Fiacha Suidhne's brother Conn was ancestor of a line of High Kings including Niall of the Nine Hostages himself. An offshoot of the line, via Colla Uais, was the progenitor of the Lords of the Isles, including the great hero Somerled, from whom the MacDonalds, MacDougalls, MacDowells and MacAlisters of the Loup claim descent. A vast swathe, therefore, of Irish and Scots surnames, proclaim high, aristocratic ancestry for countless millions of their descendants living today.

Chapter 16

WELSH AND ANCIENT BRITISH ROOTS

Welsh Research

If you are lucky, you may find your Welsh ancestors recorded in Burke's *Landed Gentry* (which includes many Welsh landed gentry families), and in Wales' vast collection of recorded pedigree material. Much of this is at The National Library of Wales (Aberystwyth, Ceredigion, Wales, SY23 3BU, www.llgc.org.uk). It holds hundreds of manuscript pedigrees, mostly coming down to about 1700.

Amongst the most detailed are the Taicroesion manuscripts of John Ellis, mainly for Gwynedd, the Alcwyn C. Evans manuscripts, mainly for south-west Wales, and the Peniarth Manuscripts. Also immensely useful are the genealogical and heraldic collections of Lewis Dwnn (or Lewys Dwynn), published as *Heraldic visitations of Wales & part of the Marches between the years 1586 & 1613, under the authority of Clarencieux & Norroy Kings at Arms, by Lewys Dwnn, Deputy Herald at Arms*, 2 vols, ed. Samuel Rush Meyrick (1846), both available at http://books.google.com. More pedigree material in other Welsh archives can be found using www.archivesnetworkwales.info/.

These collections contain masses of pedigree material, relevant to vast numbers of families of Welsh descent, or maybe all of them. The most common system of land inheritance was *gavelkind*, whereby the father's estate was divided equally between all the sons. The system resulted in large tracts of Wales being covered with tiny farms, each occupied by an impoverished descendant of a once-great landholder. In the nineteenth century, unable to scratch a living out of their tiny patches, many descendants migrated, to become coal miners, or to populate the industrial cities of the English Midlands, or the new colonies in the Americas and the Antipodes.

So, in many cases, the bloodlines exist, back from poor nineteenth-century Welsh families, to aristocratic forebears. The massive problem is making the connections. Few Welsh pedigrees state, specifically, where families lived, and few families used hereditary surnames. The problem is compounded by the maddening vagueness of the original records you will be using to trace your line back. When a nineteenth-century Welshman went to a registrar or priest to have his son registered or baptised, he knew he was John 'ap' (son of) William ap Thomas ap Lewis ap Merfyn ap Caradawg, etc., but the clerk, being trained in the English tradition of using just one surname, put him down as John Williams, with no means of distinguishing him from thousands of other men of the same names in the area.

Sometimes, with dogged persistence, it is possible to overcome the problems of too many 'Joneses' and 'Williamses' – by finding a family who stayed on the same place of land for many generations, for example, or who left wills, or who recorded themselves in a family Bible that has survived. Then, by matching up the names of each generation with the lower section of a recorded pedigree relevant to that specific place, you may be able to make a connection. But success in such cases is lamentably rare.

Though Wales seems to be lagging far behind Ireland and Scotland in this respect, it is a field set to be revolutionised by genetics. Once reliable DNA signatures can be established for the main Welsh 'Royal' and 'Nobles Lines', testing on any Welshman might establish quickly to which (if any) he belonged.

The writings of Michael Siddons on Welsh heraldry, particularly *The Development of Welsh Heraldry* (1991/1993), are highly recommended.

Making Welsh connections

Welsh genealogist Dewi Thomas is one of the many people who have found connections back through their Welsh family lines to the royal and noble tribes of Wales. A former electrical engineer in a power station, Dewi Thomas traced his family line back to John William Lloyd of Dolwuddelan, who was born in 1711. Once he had done so, he then discovered that John's ancestry had been recorded. After much work amongst the recorded Welsh pedigrees, Dewi found a line going straight back to Rhodri Mawr himself.

Many people can find routes back through English Gateway Ancestors. I found a route through my descent from the Blessed Margaret Pole. Her father George Duke of Clarence was son of Cecily, Duchess of York, whose father Ralph Nevill, Earl of Westmorland was grandson of Alice Nevill, granddaughter of Catherine Audley, whose mother Maude Giffard was daughter of Walter Clifford and Margaret, daughter of Llewellyn the Great, a Welsh prince of male-line descent from Rhodri himself.

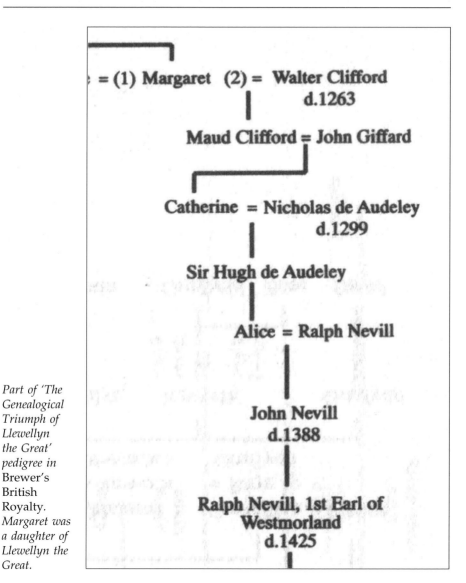

= (1) Margaret (2) = Walter Clifford
d.1263

Maud Clifford = John Giffard

Catherine = Nicholas de Audeley
d.1299

Sir Hugh de Audeley

Alice = Ralph Nevill

John Nevill
d.1388

Ralph Nevill, 1st Earl of
Westmorland
d.1425

Part of 'The Genealogical Triumph of Llewellyn the Great' pedigree in Brewer's British Royalty. *Margaret was a daughter of Llewellyn the Great.*

The Tribes of Wales

As the Angles, Saxons and Jutes pushed west across Britain in the AD 400s and 500s, the remnants of the Romano-British who were not enslaved by them retreated back, north and west. Those who ended up in the mountainous west called their new fastness Cymru, 'the land of the countrymen'. The Anglo-Saxons called them *Waelisc*, 'foreigners', and their county Wales. The Welsh called the land they had lost Loegria, 'the white land': the invaders called it Angle-land, or England.

Many Welsh genealogical lines lead back – or would, if they could be traced – to certain fixed points in the past. Welsh genealogists, from at least the time of Guttyn Owain (d. 1497), though possibly up to four centuries earlier, identified the twenty most prominent ancestors, from whom a vast number of Welsh genealogies seemed to descend. The idea was popularised in Philip Yorke's *The Royal Tribes of Wales* (1799). First are the Five Royal Tribes of Wales:

I. Griffith ap Cynan (d. 1079) King of Gwynedd (north-west Wales), descended from Anarawd, eldest son of Rhodri Mawr

II. Rhys ap Tudor (fl. 1077), King of Deheubath (south-west Wales), descended from Cadell, second son of Rhodri Mawr

III. Bleddyn ap Cynfyn, King of Powys (1046), descended from Merfyn, third son of Rhodri Mawr

IV. Ethelystan Glodrydd, tributary prince of Ferlys (between the Wye and the Severn)

V. Iestyn ap Gwrgant, tributary prince of Glamorgan

There were also 'Fifteen Noble Tribes of Wales':

I. Awfa ap Cynddellw
II. Llowarch ap Bran
III. Gweirydd ap Rhys Goch, Lord of Tal Ebolion in Anglesea
IV. Cilmin Troed Du
V. Collwyn ap Tagno, lord of Efionydel
VI. Neyfdd Harrd, Lord of Nant Conway
VII. Maeloc Crwm, Lord of Llechwedd-Isaff and Creuddyn in Carnarvon
VIII. Marchudd ap Cynan Lord of Abergelleu
IX. Hedd Molwynog, Lord of Uwch Aled
X. Braint Hir, Lord of Isdulas
XI. Marchweithian, Lord of Is-Aled
XII. Edwyn, Lord of Tegaingle, Flintshire
XIII. Ednowian Bendew, Lord of Tegaingle (fl. 1079)
XIV. Eynydd ap Gwenllian
XV. Ednowain ap Bradwen, Lord of Llys-Bradwen in Merioneth

These are male lineages. A descendant of any one of these probably has ancestors from most of the others due to intermarriage. The most

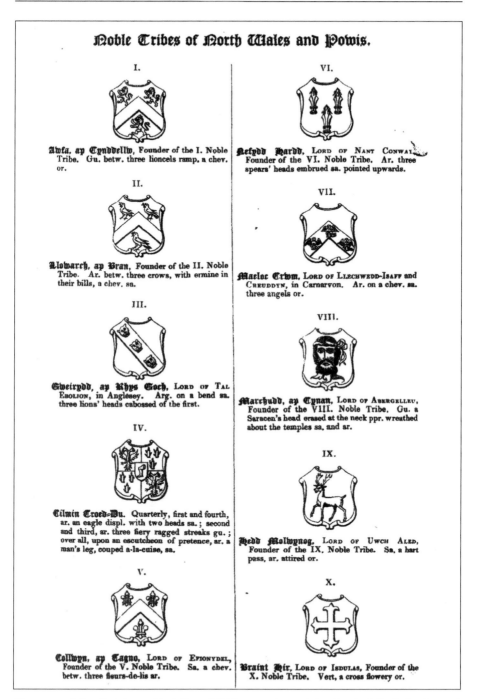

Noble Tribes of North Wales and Powis.

I.

Awfa, ap Cynddelw, Founder of the I. Noble Tribe. Gu. betw. three lioncels ramp. a chev. or.

II.

Llowarch, ap Bran, Founder of the II. Noble Tribe. Ar. betw. three crows, with ermine in their bills, a chev. sa.

III.

Gweirydd, ap Rhys Goch, Lord of Tal Ebolion, in Anglesey. Arg. on a bend sa. three lions' heads cabossed of the first.

IV.

Cilmin Troed=Du. Quarterly, first and fourth, ar. an eagle displ. with two heads sa.; second and third, ar. three fiery ragged streaks gu.; over all, upon an escutcheon of pretence, ar. a man's leg, couped a-la-cuise, sa.

V.

Collwyn, ap Tagno, Lord of Efionydel, Founder of the V. Noble Tribe. Sa. a chev. betw. three fleurs-de-lis ar.

VI.

Nefydd Hardd, Lord of Nant Conwai, Founder of the VI. Noble Tribe. Ar. three spears' heads embrued sa. pointed upwards.

VII.

Maeloc Crwm, Lord of Llechwedd-Isaff and Creuddyn, in Carnarvon. Ar. on a chev. sa. three angels or.

VIII.

Marchudd, ap Cynan, Lord of Askergelleu, Founder of the VIII. Noble Tribe. Gu. a Saracen's head erased at the neck ppr. wreathed about the temples sa. and ar.

IX.

Hedd Molwynog, Lord of Uwch Aled, Founder of the IX. Noble Tribe. Sa. a hart pass, ar. attired or.

X.

Braint Hir, Lord of Isdulas, Founder of the X. Noble Tribe. Vert, a cross flowery or.

The arms of the first ten noble tribes of Wales, as given at the front of Burke's General Armory.

exciting are the first five, which concern the royal houses ruling Wales, before Wales was subsumed by the medieval English state. The first three lineages lead back to Rhodri Mawr (d. AD 878), whom the English called 'Roderick the Great'. The son of Merfyn Frych, king of Gwynedd (north-west Wales), Rhodri extended his rule across almost all Wales, so was justly styled 'King of the Britons'.

Descents from Rhodri Mawr

A vast number of Welsh families – maybe, actually, all of them – are descended from Rhodri. So too are many non-Welsh ones, through the marriage of Welsh princesses into English families. Nesta, daughter of Gruffydd ap Llewellyn (d. 1063), married Osbern FitzRichard, the Norman lord of Richard's Castle, Herefordshire. Another daughter of Rhys ap Tudor Mawr (d. 1093), Nesta, married Gerald of Windsor. Both channelled Rhodri's blood into numerous English aristocratic families, Gerald's progeny including the FitzGeralds, Barrys and Wogans, who spawned vast, sept-like families in Ireland too.

In *Brewster's British Royalty* (1996), David Williamson published a pedigree called 'The genealogical triumph of Llewellyn the Great' (see p. 169). Llewelyn (d. 1240) was an 8 × great-grandson of Rhodri, who regained his ancestor's supremacy in Wales. His daughters married into English aristocratic families, and his blood flowed down into dynasties including the Mortimers, FitzAlans, de Bohuns, Nevills, Beauforts, Plantagenets and Tudors. Although the first Tudor king, Henry VII (d. 1509), had forced the Welsh genealogists to forge him a pedigree connecting his male-line back to Rhodri Mawr, his mother Margaret Beaufort really was descended from Rhodri, via Llewellyn.

Rhodri Mawr's Dark Age Ancestors

As Henry VII knew, to find a line of descent from Rhodri Mawr is to open a box of genealogical treats like no other, albeit with a few problems – it remains open to question, for example, whether Essylt, heiress of Gwynedd, was Merfyn Frych's wife or mother, but the latter is most likely.

Before (and after) Rhodri's time, Wales was a patchwork of small Welsh kingdoms. To try to unify Wales, Rhodri and his descendants laid considerable stress on their ancestry, through both their male line, and through their marriages to princesses who were heiresses in other parts of Wales. They formed a great collection of genealogies to prove this, which exists in two main sources, Harleian Manuscript 3859 and Jesus College, Oxford Manuscript 20. Both are printed in John Morris (ed.), *Arthurian Period Sources: Arthurian Sources*, Vol. 2, 'Genealogies and Texts' (1995) and in Peter Bartrum's *Early Welsh Genealogical Tracts* (1966).

Rhodri Mawr is therefore a Gateway Ancestor to a host of earlier Welsh royal lines. These lines descended from earlier dynasts who either claimed, or later had claimed for them, lines of descent from the *wledigs*. 'Wledig' is the Welsh term for the *duxes* (dukes), the leaders of Britain who tried to hold the country together after the Roman legions left at the start of the AD 400s, but whose power bases ended up forming the cores of the early British Dark Age kingdoms.

The first *wledig*, Coel Hen (d. *c.* AD 420) – 'Old King Cole' of the nursery rhyme – was probably a Roman commander on Hadrian's Wall. His power base in north-west England and south-west Scotland became the Kingdom of Rheged. Rhodri Mawr's father Merfyn Frych claimed male-line descent from him. Coel's daughter married the

Part of Don Pottinger's inspired pedigree of Coel Hen from Iain Moncreiffe's superb book Blood Royal *(1956), now sadly out of print, but well worth tracking down; there is a copy at the Society of Genealogists.*

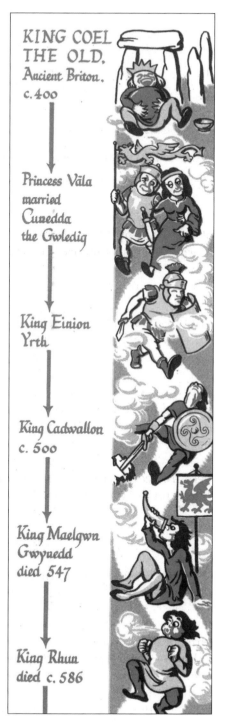

KING COEL THE OLD.
Ancient Briton.
c. 400

Princess Vâla married Cunedda the Gwledig

King Einion Yrth

King Cadwallon
c. 500

King Maelgwn Gwynedd
died 547

King Rhun
died c. 586

next *wledig*, Cunedda, who controlled south-eastern Scotland, with his base, probably, on the rock of Edinburgh. Cunedda Wledig then came down into north Wales to aid the Britons there, and his sons were claimed as ancestors by the princes of Ceredigion and Gwynedd – the ancestors of Merfyn's mother Essylt.

The *wledigs* claimed, or later had claimed for them descent from yet earlier heroes, such as Macsen Wledig, the Roman general who left Britain in the AD 380s to become Emperor of Rome, Vortigern, the proud tyrant who foolishly allowed the Jutes to settle in Kent in the first place, and his brave son Vortimer, who briefly drove them out again.

Macsen had two wives, and Rhodri Mawr was descended from sons of his by both marriages. A genealogical line connects Macsen's wife St Helen back to Bran the Blessed, whom *The Mabinogion* says was a British king living just before the Roman invasion. Though later claimed as an ancestor by Welsh kings, his capital is said to have been London, which was invaded in his absence by Cassivellaunus, a genuine, historical king of the Catuvellauni in Hertfordshire. Perhaps Bran was a real king in south-east England, who died soon before the arrival of Caesar.

The line connecting Bran down to St Helen is too short: it is not a genuine pedigree so much as a means of drawing the legendary prestige of Bran down to the descendants of Macsen and Helena. Another line – also unrealistically short – goes back from Macsen's wife Keindrech to Beli Mawr, a semi-mythical king of the Catuvellauni in Hertfordshire in the first century BC: he was the purported father of Cassivellaunus and of Lud, builder (or rebuilder?) of London, and a great-great-grandfather of Caratacus.

Both Coel and Cunedda also had pedigrees claiming male-line descent from Beli Mawr. These were surely not true, but they are fascinating as insights into how the Dark Age Britons viewed their history, and how they used genealogy to bolster their political standing.

Their genealogical claims went yet further, for Beli Mawr, they claimed, had married Anna, daughter of Joseph of Arimathea, the uncle of the Virgin Mary.

Joseph of Arimathea was said to have married the daughter of Longinus, the Roman legionary who pierced the side of Christ on the cross, and who was himself (they said) an illegitimate son of Julius Caesar. After Christ's death, he, several Apostles and Mary Magdalene were believed to have travelled to France, and Joseph was

174

then believed to have come to Glastonbury in Somerset. From this arose that wonderful story that Joseph had also visited Glastonbury many years earlier – bringing with him the child Jesus, whose feet, 'in ancient times', as Blake wrote in *Jerusalem*, walked 'upon England's mountains green'.

None of it was true, and the dates don't really work anyway. But these myths were not the work of irresponsible genealogists, meddling with history. What we have here are the dreams of Dark Age Britons, deeply committed to Christianity, yet painfully aware of how far removed their land was from the events in the Bible. Through the myth of Joseph, they sought merely to find their place in the Biblical narrative. The genealogical conceit of the Welsh princes, who claimed that Biblical blood flowed in their veins, was an almost inevitable result of the myth-making process.

Rhodri Mawr's Iron Age Ancestors

As if these stories were not enough, Bran the Blessed and Beli Mawr had fabulous male-line ancestries too. They appear in Peter Bartrum's *Early Welsh Genealogical Tracts* (1966). Pedigrees such as *Bonedd yr Arwyr* ('the Descents of the Heroes') and *Brenhinllwuth Morganwc*, the pedigree of the Dark Age kings of Morganwg (Glamorgan), show virtually identical descents for Bran from Brutus, the mythological Trojan founder of Britain.

Gruffydd ap Cynan (d. 1137), the great-grandfather of Llewellyn the Great, and a 5 × great-grandson of Rhodri Mawr, also had a pedigree, *Hanes* [History of] *Gruffydd ap Cynan*, which claimed that Beli Mawr was descended from Brutus too, and there are other pedigrees connecting Beli to Brutus, by different routes. One of these appears in narrative form in Geoffrey of Monmouth's *History of the Kings of Britain* (*c*. 1135), one of the most widely read and widely believed books in medieval England.

In the 1190s, Gerald of Wales wrote of such descents, and the way he writes suggests they had existed for considerably more than the last fifty years:

> You have to bear in mind that the Welsh bards, singers and jongleurs kept accurate copies of the genealogies of these princes [of north and south Wales] in their old manuscripts, which are, of course, written in Welsh. They would recite them from memory, going back from Rhodri Mawr to the time of the Blessed Virgin

King Lud, son of Beli Mawr, with his sons Androgeus and Tasciovanus, at St Dunstan-in-the-West, London. These figures in Britain's royal genealogy hover on the border between reality and myth.

Mary [whose first cousin Anna was believed to have married Beli Mawr], and then further still to [Brutus' father] Silvius, Ascanius and Aeneas. They then continue the line back to Adam himself.

The Ancestry of Bran the Blessed

It seems as if the different versions of Beli's ancestry were worked up between the time of Nennius in the early 800s and the 1130s. Their purpose was to fill the awkward gap between Beli, in about 100 BC, and Brutus, who lived only three generations after the Trojan War (*c.* 1194–1184 BC). Each version is an experiment, some far too short to do the job properly, and one can see the same sections of names appearing in different places in different pedigrees. The implication is that the different strands of pedigrees being used had already existed. This begs a fascinating question – perhaps British genealogy's 'million dollar' question: of the strands of pedigrees being used in such pedigrees, were any of them genuinely old, Iron Age tribal pedigrees? No such pedigrees have survived in their own right, but are some hidden here, before our eyes, amongst the fabricated descents of Beli Mawr from Brutus?

Scholars including the great archaeologist Sir Flinders Petrie have considered such questions in the past, but tended to become polarised, either insisting that the pedigrees were entirely accurate or were complete fantasy. But tribal pedigrees, transmitted orally, then in writing, copied and miscopied and then manipulated to fulfil a purpose for which they were not originally intended can fall between these two extremes.

Bran's ancestry, in *Bonedd yr Arwyr*, is:

Bran; Llyr Lleteith; Garar; Gerein Hir; Secuyn; Keit; Arth; Morunan; Kerint; Cridol; Dingarth; Annun; Lainus; Brutus.

Before it was used to connect back to Brutus and his son Lainus (a garbled form of Locrinus) this may have been a genuine pedigree of a south-eastern tribal dynasty, going back to Annun. The *Hanes Gruffydd ap Cynan* offers a clue that there may be a couple of missing generations here, because it continues a line back from 'Dyvynarth' (identical with Dingarth, above) to 'Prydain; Aedd Mawr; Antonius', where Antonius is the equivalent of 'Annun'. So the 'original' pedigree may have been more like:

Bran; Llyr Lleteith; Garar; Gerein Hir; Secuyn; Keit; Arth; Morunan; Kerint; Cridol; Dingarth; Prydain; Aedd Mawr; Annun.

Prydain son of Aedd Mawr appears independently in a bardic triad (a three-line poem) in the *Red Book of Hergest* as a heroic, eponymous conqueror of Britain. 'Aedd Mawr' means 'great fire', and he and Annun were probably gods, perhaps equivalents of Zeus and Kronos. It may have been from such heroes and gods that the rulers of south-eastern Britain had once claimed descent.

The Ancestry of Beli Mawr

Beli Mawr's Catuvellauni ancestors were incoming conquerors, who (as *The Mabinogion* relates) eventually overran Bran's realm. *Hanes Gruffydd ap Cynan* makes Beli son of Manogan, 'son' of Eneit, son of Kerwyt, who was identical with Kerint in the pedigree above. Geoffrey of Monmouth's *History of the Kings of Britain*, however, identifies Beli's father as Diguellus. But what if Manogan was Beli's *mother*? Then, the pedigree may have recorded a claim by the Catuvellauni, resulting from a marriage alliance, to be descended from the same ancestors as Bran – and thus to have some hereditary claim to his kingdom. Admittedly, Beli's pedigree is rather shorter than Bran's, but perhaps a couple of generations are missing: I do not seek to prove a case here, but merely to suggest how these apparently chaotic pedigrees could possibly make sense.

The Welsh pedigrees link Beli back to Brutus using Manogan's descent from Dingarth/Dyvynarth, as above. Some versions, such as *Hanes*, lengthen the period covered by splicing extra generations in before Annun/'Antonius'. These go back in *Hanes* as follows:

Antonius [Annun]; Seiroel; Gurust; Riwallaun; Kunedda; Regat; llyr; Rud; Bleidud; Lliwelyt; Brutus Ysgwyt Ir; Evrog; Membyr; Madauc; Llocrinus; Brut[us].

Is this a genuinely old pedigree, and if so of whom? Geoffrey of Monmouth repeats a similar list, coming down from Brutus, and includes their stories: Llyr was Geoffrey's (and later Shakespeare's) King Leir, and Regat was Regan, one of his faithless daughters. Geoffrey turns them into rulers of all Britain and claims, surely falsely, that they founded well-known cities all over the island, but he includes Bladud (Bleidud) founding Bath, and Rud founding Shaftesbury. These were scarcely places of any consequence in Geoffrey's time, but we now know that both were of Iron Age origin (Bath having originated with the hill fort of Little Solsbury Hill).

Ebraucus (Evrog), meanwhile, founded 'the city of Mount Agned which is now called the Maiden's Castle', but I suspect that 'now called' is a mistake, and two places had been intended: Nennius calls the Somerset hill fort of South Cadbury 'Agned Cathregonion', and 'Maiden's Castle' is the name of the great hill fort close to Dorchester, Dorset. Both South Cadbury and Maiden Castle are of similar design, and date from about the 400s BC.

The Iron Age hill fort of Little Solsbury Hill above Bath, said to have been founded by Bladud – who may possibly have been a genuine Iron Age Durotrige/Dobunni ruler.

If we recognise Brutus and his son as later additions, and remove them, we may have here a pedigree of a south-western tribal dynasty, which at different times covered the tribal areas of the Durotiges of Dorset and southern Somerset and the Dobunni of northern Somerset and Gloucestershire. Geoffrey is often accused of wild invention, but the Welsh pedigrees show he had not invented the names here: perhaps some credibility can be attached to his references to West Country places after all.

After Sisillus (Seiroel), incidentally, Geoffrey describes the reigns of Gorbudoc and his sons Ferrex and Porrex, after which there was a terrible war. Gorbudoc's name is oddly similar to Bodvoc, whose coins appear in Dobunni territory towards the end of the first century BC. Ferrex and Porrex seem also to echo Catti and Comux, a pair of contemporary Dobunni rulers, who appear on coins there in the early first century AD, at the time when Belgae, kinsmen of the Catuvellauni, were making bloody inroads into the south-west.

179

If there is some historical basis for this south-western pedigree, there may be some reality to the story of King Leir. We hear of him using French help to regain his throne from his feckless older daughters. Did the original story relate that he called in help from Gaul? Was it Leir who inadvertently caused the Belgic invasion of south-western England?

In Geoffrey's narrative, the story of the foregoing kings ends with a terrible war, after which a new dynasty gains the 'British' throne. Its descendants included Diguellus and his son 'Heli' (Beli Mawr). This line does not appear in the surviving Welsh sources and so is unique to Geoffrey. It may be completely made up, but (unlike Geoffrey) we know the Catuvellauni ancestors of Beli Mawr were from northern France, so it is perhaps beyond coincidence that many of the adventures of these supposedly 'British' kings actually took place in Gaul.

Geoffrey's story focuses on Brennius and Belinus. This parallels Livy's account of the Gaulish attack on Rome, led by 'Brennus', in about 390 BC, but Geoffrey's version is told (and wildly exaggerated) from the point of view of the invaders. Geoffrey's list of names between Brennius and Diguellus is far too long – but this is because Geoffrey's main intention was simply to fill the gap between Brutus and Beli. The list seems to have been padded out with a section of names, between Capoir and Catellus, written in distinctly different style. If these are indeed an interpolation, and are removed, then Geoffrey's pedigree goes:

Heli [Beli Mawr]; Diguellus; Capoir; [...]; Catellus; Gerennius; Elidurus; Morvidius; Danius; Sisillus [not the same one as mentioned above]; Guithelin; Gurguit; Belinus [brother of Brennius]; Dunvallo; Cloten.

This produces a plausible number of generations from Beli back to the 390s BC, and includes the intriguing name Catellus, perhaps an eponym for the Catuvellauni. There is a whisper of a chance that, amongst all Geoffrey's embellishments and additions, he has preserved the skeleton of a genuine tribal pedigree of the Iron Age Catuvellauni tribe. The likelihood that they were really descended from Brennus the Gaul who besieged Rome is minimal, but it is not entirely implausible as the sort of drunken brag one might expect from a late Iron Age Belgic chieftain.

If Beli existed, and was son of Diguellus, a Catuvellauni king in Hertfordshire, and his wife Manogan, a princess from Bran's native dynasty of south-east England, it should not surprise us. Beli's great-great-grandson Caratacus was taken as a prisoner to Rome, and there was ample opportunity for his ancestry to have been recorded, and to have survived (albeit unknown to Nennius) down to Geoffrey's time. It may have included the pedigree of Leir and Bladud too, who were perhaps ancestors of Caratacus's family through another marriage alliance.

Bladud, whose statue has recently been restored to the Parade Gardens, Bath.

For all we know, both Bran and Beli Mawr may be purely mythical figures, and all the pedigree material before them could just be the result of Dark Age imaginings. But when dissected in this way, and considered as tribal, not national pedigrees, they attain at least some semblance of plausibility. Who knows: they may even be partly genuine.

Nobody exploring their ancient Welsh and British ancestry can expect to find pedigrees that are soberly, historically accurate. But the pedigrees that do survive provide a fabulous insight into the mindsets of our pre-medieval British ancestors, revealing how they used genealogy to further their political and religious aspirations and to express the extraordinary dreams they had about their own origins.

But such dreams were not restricted to the Britons. As we shall see in the next chapter, the Germanic invaders of Britain were no more sober when it came to their genealogical imaginations.

Chapter 17

SAXONS, VIKINGS AND NORMANS

Angles, Saxons and Jutes

Even before the Roman legions left Britain at the start of the AD 400s, Saxons were coming to the south-east as hired mercenaries, and settling there. Once the Empire began to fragment, the Saxons assumed ever increasing power, and encouraged their kinsman to leave their homes in Holland, north Germany and Denmark and come over in their longboats. Neighbouring tribes, the Angles and Jutes, joined in the free-for-all, and over the next few centuries they formed kingdoms in Angle-land, 'England'. The Romano-British were either enslaved, or killed, or retreated ever west, into Cornwall (and thence Brittany, 'little Britain'), Strathcylde and Wales.

Many English families are of Anglo-Saxon origin, but it is very unusual indeed to be able to prove an unbroken male line back to an Anglo-Saxon who had lived before the Norman Conquest. The Englefields of Englefield, Berkshire can do so, as can the Ardens (the ancestors of Shakespeare's mother), but they are few and far between. The 'Prosopography of Anglo-Saxon England' project, www.pase.a-c.uk/index.html, is a database to Anglo-Saxons whose names have survived in records – and to whom new genealogical links might yet be found.

Through Gateway Ancestors, there are a number of solid Anglo-Saxon connections via female lines. Henry I (d. 1135) of England married Matilda, daughter of Malcolm III, King of Scots (d. 1093): her mother was St Margaret, daughter of Edward Atheling, son of Edmund Ironside (d. 1016), one of the last Saxon kings of England and a descendant of Alfred the Great. Another line comes down from Harold II, who was slain at Hastings, whose daughter Gytha was mother of Mstislav-Harold, Grand Duke of Kiev: their daughter married Geza II of Hungary, whose great-granddaughter married James I of Aragon, whose daughter married Philip III of France, whose granddaughter married Edward II of England.

It was Alfred the Great (d. 899) who expanded his kingdom of Wessex to unify England under one crown. Earlier, the land had been divided between the Heptarchy, the 'seven' Anglo-Saxon kingdoms – though there were actually more – Wessex, Mercia, Northumbria and Bernicia, Deira, East Anglia, Essex, Sussex and Kent. The genealogies of these dynasties were recorded in Nennius' *History of the Britons* and the *Anglo-Saxon Chronicle*. They are discussed in Kenneth Sisnam's 'Anglo-Saxon Royal Genealogies', *Proceedings of the British Academy* (1953), 287–348 (a bound copy is at the Society of Genealogists). *Brewster's British Royalty* (1996) gives good pedigrees of them too.

The Anglo-Saxons kings' genealogists recorded their genuine descent from Continental chieftains. The kings of Mercia, for example, claimed descent from Wermund, a genuine king of the Angles in Jutland, Denmark, in about AD 350. Back beyond their genuine forebears, all the dynasties claimed descent from Odin or Woden, the king of the gods in the northern world.

Ironically, the dynastic pedigree least likely to be true is that of Wessex itself. Its founder Cerdic was supposedly of good, Continental Saxon stock, yet his name was obviously British – it is a variant of Caratacus. Cerdic was probably a Romano-Briton, though perhaps with a Saxon mother, who talked-up his Saxon credentials as power shifted, and whose descendants later fabricated the Saxon genealogy we now have for him.

The Franks

Taking the line of the Kings of Wessex back through Alfred the Great we reach his great-grandfather Ealhmund, King of Wessex, who married a daughter of Ethelbert II, King of Kent. Ethelbert II's great-great-grandfather Eadbald, King of Kent married Emma, a French Merovingian princess. Eadbald's mother Bertha was also a Merovingian, who was largely instrumental in the introduction of Christianity to England.

Bertha's father was Charibert, King of Paris, a grandson of Clovis and a great-great-grandson of Merovech, founder of the dynasty. Merovech was a Frankish king whose tribal, godly origins were deliberately expunged when his family converted to Christianity. Later, the *Liber Historiae Francorum* (c. AD 720s) deduced him, inventively, from Markomir, a hitherto unheard of son of Priam, King of Troy at the time of the Trojan War. Much more recently, Michael Baigent, Richard Leigh and Henry Lincoln's sensationalist *The Holy Blood and the Holy Grail* (1996) deduced Merovech, equally fancifully, but with far less poetic justification, from the family of Jesus Christ himself.

Vikings and Normans

In the north lands, the ancient gods known in Greece as Gaia (Mother Earth) and Zeus (king of the gods), had their equivalents in Freya ('our lady', also called Nerthus) and Odin (or Woden). Freya was ancestress of the godly family of the Vanir, whilst from Odin descended the Vanir's warring rivals, the Aesir.

All dynasties across the Germanic, Anglo-Saxon and Norse world claimed either Freya or Odin as their ancestors, and were known, respectively, as Ynglings, with their sacred capital at Uppsala, Sweden, and Skiöldungs. The latter were named after Odin's son Scyld and had their base at Lethra (Lejra), a stone circle on the Danish island of Sjaelland (Zealand). Both were originally sacral kingships, whereby the king was seen as an incarnation of his godly ancestor, and was sacrificed at the end of his term of kingship – as Odin says in the *Hávamál* poem, 'myself a sacrifice to myself'.

Most Anglo-Saxon dynasties were Skiöldungs, claiming Odin as their ancestor, whilst their northern neighbours, the Vikings, generally claimed to be Ynglings. Thus, the Kings of Norway were Ynglings, and from their younger branches came the Dukes of Normandy, the Jarls or Earls of Orkney and the Viking kings of York, Dublin and the Western Isles of Scotland. However, the Viking dynasty of Ivar Wide-Fathom, who supplanted the Ynglings in Uppsala in about AD 690, claimed to be Skiöldungs: from them descended the royal house of Denmark, including Harald III Blue-Tooth, Sweyn Fork-Beard and Canute the Great, whose rule extended over much of Dark Age England as well.

Under Christian influence, the Trojan myth spread to the Vikings, and chroniclers started inventing genealogies for Odin and Freya back to the family of Priam, King of Troy.

Vast numbers of British families have aristocratic Viking ancestry. In Scotland, the Jarls (earls) of Orkney are ancestral to many families through female lines: Ingrid, daughter of Jarl St Ragnvald III (d. 1158) married Erik Straybrails and had a daughter Ragnhild, wife of Gunni Andresson, from whom descends the Clan Gunn. Another daughter of Ingrid was probably wife of Gillebride, Earl of Angus, and thus ancestress of the Ogilvies. Jarl Haakon of Orkney (d. 1126) had a daughter Ingborg, wife of her Yngling cousin Olaf I Bitling, King of the Isles (d. 1153). They had a daughter Ragnhailt, wife of the famous warlord Somerled (d. 1164), Lord of the Isles, ancestor of the MacDonalds. Olaf's aunt Helga of the Beautiful Locks, meanwhile, was mother of Gillemuire, ancestor of Leod, founder of the MacLeods.

The Vikings who settled in northern France became Normans, and came flooding across the Channel in 1066. The Normans founded numerous aristocratic dynasties in England and, later, in Wales, Ireland and Lowland Scotland. As the Conquest grew more distant, it came to be seen as a satisfactory starting point for any English genealogy. It served, like the Great Flood or the Trojan War, as a dividing line between the distant past, and the here and now, and for the unhistorically minded what went before became irrelevant. Thus, numerous pedigrees were extended back from the earliest genuine ancestor to a yet earlier one who 'came over with the Conqueror'.

The Battle Abbey Roll, with some account of the Norman Lineages, 3 vols (1889) was a well-meaning attempt by the Duchess of Cleveland to collate all these claims. It includes much genuine information, but her work gave a new veneer of authenticity to a lot of pure fantasy. Horace Round demolished many of the *Roll's* false pedigrees, and more recently Anthony Camp organised a massive 'clean-up' through his book *My ancestor came over with the Conqueror, those who did, and some of those who probably did not* (1988).

The genuine Norman origins of many prominent English families are discussed in Sir Anthony Wagner's *English Genealogy* (1983). His *Pedigree and Progress* (1975) includes pedigrees showing the descent of the leading Norman dynasts from the extended family of the Conqueror himself, particularly through the illegitimate offspring of William's great-grandfather Duke Richard I (d. 996) and the sisters of Richard's concubine Gunnor. From Duke Richard's bastards, for example, came an extended web including the de Clares, de Montforts and the Dukes of Brittany and Richmond, whilst from Gunnor's kin came the Warennes, Montgomerys, Beaumonts and Giffords.

Through these families, and many more, the blood of the Vikings, with their legendary claims to descent from Freya and Odin, and thus from King Priam of Troy, was disseminated amongst innumerable English families. And Priam, as we know from Homer, was descended from Zeus. But how is it possible for human lineages to start with gods? Where does reality end and myth begin?

Epilogue

'MY ANCESTOR WAS A GOD!'

Encountering the Gods

As we trace back to the earliest royal lines, odd things start happening. Humans give way, it seems, to gods.

What was going on? Why did so many genealogical lines depart from human history and blossom into the supernatural?

This is a part of the subject that all experienced genealogists know about, but few like to talk about. Yet to me this is the most fascinating part of genealogy, and takes us to the heart of our love affair with the subject. It also helps answer the question with which we started this book – what it is about aristocratic ancestors that exerts such an enduring attraction on so many people?

Before we had mapped out the evolution of humans from apes, and ultimately from the earliest living organisms, and then the entire history of the Earth and the Universe itself, we relied on the supernatural to account for the vast span of time between the start of the world and the written or remembered history of our particular nations and families.

The Australian Aboriginals continued a belief system that was perhaps what all hunter-gatherers, including those of Ice Age Europe, once believed. They had no use for long genealogies, and indeed dead ancestors' names were strictly taboo. The world was born in the Dreamtime, in whose timeless vastness dwelt all the ancestors, and the animal spirits that animated the universe. Beyond the immediate relationships within the small hunter-gatherer bands, broader social cohesion was achieved by each person seeking out their 'animal ancestor' through visions, and then encountering other people from different bands, who shared this same spiritual progenitor. Such vision-ancestors also rooted each person, simply and directly, in a spiritual being that inhabited the eternal Dreamtime.

When farming came, it gave rise to gods, first half-animal, half-human and then fully human – first mother goddesses, then, much later, all-powerful gods. As villages and cities grew older and the

187

skulls of dead generations piled up, it became harder to deny that human history had lasted for more than a handful of generations: genealogies started being remembered, and King Lists started being recorded.

Early kings, such as those in Mesopotamia, made regular, ritual marriages with goddesses (who were conveniently believed to inhabit the bodies of temple priestesses). The king was thus the consort of the goddess, and his offspring were semi-divine. A memory of this survives, in Homer's story of Aeneas, the Trojan prince who was born from the union of the mortal Anchises and the goddess Aphrodite.

Thus, early royal pedigrees started with, and were constantly regenerated by, the union of men and goddesses. As the goddess was immortal, she accounted for all time – the equivalent of the Aborigines' Dreamtime – which had gone before. And just as hunter-gatherer relationships were determined by common connection to the same animal ancestor, so too were relationships between tribes and cities cemented by a shared belief in descent from the same deity, or a perceived genealogical connection between different ancestral deities – and wars were justified, of course, by quarrels between those godly ancestors in Heaven.

Long after the practice of direct unions between kings and priestesses symbolising deities had ended, royal descents from deities remained fundamentally important to national identity, accounting for political supremacy, and defining the relationship between nations and the otherwise giddying sweep of time.

The ancient Greeks deduced their royal lines from heroes, born from the union of humans and deities. Hesiod (c. 700s BC), the first genealogist, defined the interrelationships of the gods in his *Theogony*, and his Olympian genealogy was extended down to human level in the *Hesiodic Catalogue of Women* (c. 530s BC). Hesiod mentions, casually, that even his family was descended from Zeus (and thus shows himself to have been no different to anyone you might find lurking about the library of the Society of Genealogists, terribly proud of their ancestry and always keen to drop a few details into the conversation). Alexander the Great (d. 323 BC) believed his father was descended from Hercules, son of Zeus, and that his mother was descended from Achilles, descendant both of Zeus and the Titan deity of the Ocean. These pedigrees were made up, but the confidence they inspired in Alexander carried him all the way to India.

The Romans had similar beliefs in the descent of their rulers from gods: Romulus, their founding hero, was the son of Mars, the battle-god. When Alexander's young cousin Pyrrhus of Epirus made war on Rome, he likened the struggle to that of his ancestor Achilles against the Trojans. When Pyrrhus lost, the Romans proudly announced that they, the Trojans, had won, and adopted an existing Greek story that Aeneas had escaped from Troy and settled on their shores. Aeneas was made into the ancestor of Romulus' mother, and Virgil immortalised the new tradition in the *Aeneid*. Many patrician Roman families started claiming Trojan ancestry: Varro's tragically lost *De Familiis Troianis*, the spiritual ancestor of *Burke's Peerage*, recorded them all. The Gens Julii, the family of Caesar, even claimed Aeneas himself as the father of their eponymous ancestor, Iulus. This pedigree was made up, but the confidence it inspired in Caesar carried him to Britain.

Adam and Eve

Christianity changed everything. The Bible's genealogical structure, whether inspired by God or the work of Hesiod, deduced all humans back to Noah, who survived the Great Flood. Jesus alone was born of the union of a human and the deity, but Noah's ancestor Adam was created when the world began, by God.

Any nation adopting Christianity had to cut itself adrift from its traditional gods, and thus from the way it had rooted itself in time. New routes had to be found – there is an almost palpable sense of panic in the process – to Noah. Often, nations achieved this by euhemerising their gods – saying that they were not divinities, but merely ancient, heroic humans – and then connecting them back to Noah.

The trouble was that the Bible, as a written record, showed many generations going back to Noah's time. Writing was still new to Western Europe, and the tribal genealogies did not stretch back nearly far enough (very few orally transmitted genealogies go back much before twenty generations: not even bards have endless memories).

One solution was to graft tribal genealogies onto the palpably older genealogies of the classical world. One favoured route was the Trojan pedigree. It started with Dardanos, son of Zeus, and came down to Priam, who was king at the time of the Trojan War, and his cousin Anchises, the father of Aeneas. As the Dark Ages progressed, Zeus was euhemerised into a human king, descended from Noah, and lines were imagined down from Priam to the gods of the Saxons and

Vikings, and from Aeneas to the High Kings of Ireland and the tribal rulers of Wales.

With Ireland, we must be cautious, for only the vestige of a story deducing the Gaels from Aeneas remains, in the *Life of St Cadroe* (c. AD 900s), but remain it does, with his son Iulus already half-disguised as Niulum. Later versions spun out a long pedigree of Gaelic names from the son, who is often simply 'Nel', down to Milesius, whose sons Heber and Heremon were said to have colonised Ireland: Aeneas became 'Feinius Farsaidh', his original ancestors forgotten and substituted with a further line of Gaelic names to connect him back to Noah. The final version, in the *Lebor Gabála Érenn*, is barely recognisable as a Trojan story, save that it concerns the westerly travels of heroic ancestors from the eastern Mediterranean. As a means of linking Ireland to the land of the Bible, it was – and remains – enduringly powerful.

Brutus of Troy

A parallel Welsh process resulted in the imagining of an eponymous ancestor of the British, Brutus, who was made into a grandson of Aeneas's son Ascanius. His name was originally 'Britto', and handily echoed Bruide, the royal name of the Pictish kings, and it evolved into 'Brutus' because of the name's Roman overtones.

The process began in the AD 600s (Nennius quotes a pedigree of Brutus by St Cuanu, who died in AD 640) and the story was widely accepted when Nennius recorded several versions of it in about AD 820. Soon, British tribal genealogies had been spun out to create a convincing connection back from the contemporary rulers of Wales to Brutus, and hence to Aeneas, Dardanos, Zeus, Noah and thus to Adam, whom God had made in his own likeness.

The Welsh princes and their people had regained the security their pagan ancestors had enjoyed before Christianity came: they knew their connection back to the divine, and how they stood in relation to the vast sweep of universal history – and with a prestigious connection with the founder of Rome thrown in too.

In the 1130s, Geoffrey of Monmouth's *History of the Kings of Britain* worked Brutus's story up into a short epic with Virgilian overtones. He told how Brutus had freed many Trojans enslaved in Epirus, and led them to Devon, where they landed at Totnes, battled against the giants who inhabited Britain, and settled the land. The island yielded

William Blake's picture The landing of Brutus in England, *in which Brutus kneels to kiss the shore at Totnes, captures vividly the spiritual essence of the Brutus myth, and the sacred union between the Trojans and the soil of Britain. (Princeton University Library)*

its fertile riches to Brutus and his successors, who became the ancestors of the Britons (and thus of the Welsh).

These stories, the Milesian origins of the Irish (and thus of the Scots) and the founding of Britain by Brutus, lay at the start of all chronicle histories of Ireland (and Scotland) and of southern Britain, respectively, throughout the Middle Ages. They rooted those nations in time, and connected them back to Adam and Eve. English invasions of its neighbours were justified on the grounds that Geoffrey's Brutus had made London his capital and granted Wales and Scotland to younger sons. Henry VII sent a commission to Wales to 'discover' his male-line descent from the Welsh princes, so as to be able to proclaim himself the descendant, and heir, of Brutus, and up until James I's time such claims lay at the heart of royal self-image.

The genealogist Thomas Lyte presented James with a huge pedigree, over 6ft by 8ft in size and brightly illuminated in vivid reds, blues and gold. At its head was depicted James and his family.

191

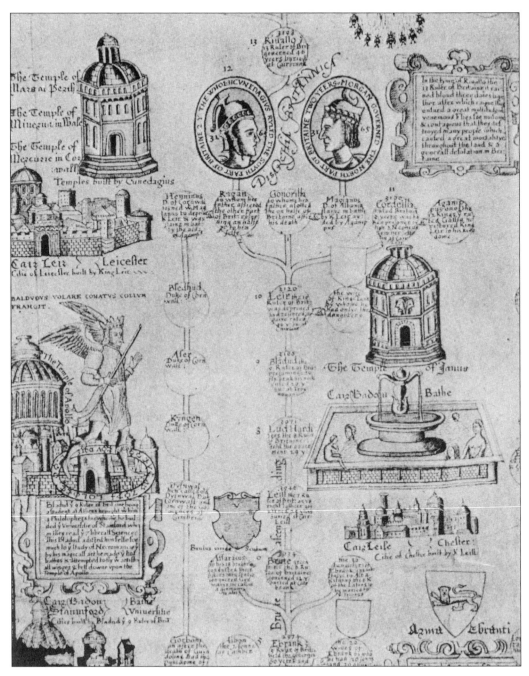

Part of Thomas Lyte's great pedigree of James I, showing some of Britain's early mythologised kings, including Bladud (a descendant of Brutus), founder of Bath, who died attempting to fly with artificial wings.

Up the centre of the chart rose the 'Imperial line' from the Normans, joined by the Tudors: on the sides were James's other illustrious descents – from the Saxons and their founder Odin, the legendary Irish ancestors of the Kings of the Scots and Brutus, descendant of Adam and Eve.

Yet whilst the Stuart court marvelled, there were mutterings. All such fabulous pedigrees are contrived, made up over 2,000 years' worth of written tradition. Unlike the fluid genealogies of pre-literate tribes, where the deity and the start of the world could hover a score or two generations before the present without fear of contradiction, written myths can be dissected and over-analysed, and be found to be wanting.

Back in 1534, the Renaissance Humanist scholar Polydore Vergil had argued that Brutus was a mere story. By the mid-seventeenth century few people were left in Britain who took the Trojan myth seriously. Philip Stanhope, Earl of Chesterfield (d. 1713) famously lampooned all such myths by hanging up two portraits in his London house. One was labelled 'Adam de Stanhope' and the other 'Eve de Stanhope'.

As with the onset of Christianity, which swept away so many comforting pagan myths, there is a sense of deep crisis in the intellectual life of Tudor and Stuart Britain. If traditional pedigrees were false, and the nations' connection back to Adam was a fable, then what was the truth? The portals of time flew open, and our ancestors found themselves staring straight into a gaping abyss of time. For many, like Chesterfield, sarcastic humour was the only resort left to cope with the shock.

The answer was antiquarianism, archaeology, the meticulous picking over of traces of the past, to try to reconstruct a new, scientifically justified story. Science itself developed apace, questing for the origins of humanity, and the origins of the universe. Sir Francis Bacon, Sir Isaac Newton, Charles Darwin, Stephen Hawking and countless others have pieced together a story that is broadly convincing – though many people still prefer the genealogies in the Bible. In doing so, they sought to replace everything that was lost when Brutus of Troy was cashiered by Polydore Vergil.

With the loss of Brutus, genealogy, which once lay at the very heart of royal, national and human self-consciousness, was marginalised. Genealogists went about soberly pruning the gods, the heroes and the family of Adam off the tops of their pedigrees – and were then left wondering why their subject no longer exerted such a powerful fascination as it had done in the past. Luckily, they did not wholly succeed in drowning the subject in mundanity, for the older pedigrees survived, and at the tops, the heroes of old remain.

Having thus journeyed through the history of genealogy, maybe we should no longer feel surprised at the appearance of gods and heroes at the tops of old royal pedigrees. Perhaps we should feel more surprised that anybody since the seventeenth century could possibly have been satisfied with pedigrees that *don't* go back as far. The sanitised versions may be truer to human history, but it is in the older pedigrees that we find the mythological connections between ourselves and the songs of Homer and verses of Virgil – a formidable counterpoise to the materialism of the modern era. And the old pedigrees capped by gods tell us an enormous amount about how our ancestors viewed themselves and their relationship with time.

It is to the very fine world of mythology that the bloodlines of the aristocracy, and of early royalty, connect our culture, and all of us. If you can find your own direct blood link back to that world of mythical marvels via your own aristocratic ancestry, then so much the better for you.

The belief that early royalty was descended from gods provides, at last, the answer to the question with which we started this book – what is it that makes aristocratic ancestry so special? In part it is simply that aristocratic lines are usually much better recorded, and go further back, than non-noble ones. It is also because, through Gateway Ancestors, they lead back to royal lines, which generally go back even further.

Ultimately, however, these royal lines, to which so many of us are connected by lines of aristocratic ancestry, take that extra step back, not to real, human ancestors, but to kings and queens who claimed descent from Adam, from heroes, from gods. Through such time-honoured claims, those elevated beings become *our* ancestors as well. It is this aura of divinity that raised kings above normal people, in the early days of civilisation. It created a golden light that bathed them and their descendants in glory: a light that continues to shine down their long pedigrees, to this very day – right down to us.

Envoi

... and if you have yet to find your own aristocratic ancestors, and thus your personal links back to this genealogical wonderland, then I wish you, as the Duke of Somerset once wished me, very 'good hunting'!

SELECT INDEX

Aboriginal Australians, 9, 187–8
Achilles, 4, 142, 188–9
Adam and Eve, 3, 119–21, 131, 149, 163, 176, 189–91, 193–4
Aedd Mawr, 177
Aeneas and the *Aeneid*, 3–4, 39, 70, 129, 160, 162–3, 176, 188–90
Aesir, dynasty, 185
Agathyrsus, son of Hercules, 160
Alexander the Great, 134, 142–3, 188–9
Alfred the Great, 183–4
Almanach de Gotha, 145
Anderson, James, 131
Anglo-Saxon Chronicle, 184
Anjou, Counts of, 129
Aphrodite, 3, 188
Apothecaries, Society of, 104
Aquitaine, Dukes of, 149
Armenia, 124, 140–3
arms, coats of, 14, 17, 21, 26–7, 39–51, 68–9, 71, 74, 95, 109
Arthur, king, 3, 57, 173
Ascanius, 176, 190
Atlantic Modal Haplotype, 119, 133
Augustus, emperor, 52–3

Balfour Paul, Sir James, 49, 85
Bank of England, 105
Bannatyne Club, 106
Bartrum, Peter, 173, 175
bastardy bonds, 29, 96
Battle Abbey Roll, 186
Beauclerk-Dewar, Peter, 137
Bedwell, Nancy, 115
Belgae, 161–2, 179
Beli Mawr, 174–8, 180, 182
Betham, William, 131
Betts of Wortham Hall, Suffolk, 122–3
Bierbrier, M.L., 143
Bigland, Ralph, 76

birthbrieves, 79
Bladud/Bleidud, legendary founder of Bath, 178–9, 181, 192
Blake, William, 175, 191
Blomefield, Revd Francis, 74
Boccaccio, Giovanni, 5, 7
Bond surname 36, 137
Bonedd yr Arwyr, 175, 177
Borgia, 149
Bortrick, William, 131
Boyd Roberts, Gary, 136
Bran the Blessed, 174–6
Brennus the Gaul, 180
Brewster's British Royalty, 172, 184
Brian Boru, High King of Ireland, 163
Bride/Bruide/Brigid, 160, 190
Brittany, Dukes of, 155, 183, 186
Browne, Sir Anthony, 133
Bruce, 36, 155–6
Brutus of Troy, 70–1, 80, 129, 175–80, 190–3
Brydges, Sir Egerton, 82
Burke's family and publications, 1, 2, 24–7, 29–31, 46, 58–60, 62, 65–7, 82–94, 110, 131–4, 144–5, 149, 152, 167, 171, 189
Buttriss, Jacquie, 150
Byzantium, emperors of, 140–1, 147–8

Cambridge, William and Kate, Duke and Duchess of, 1, 49–51, 128, 139
Camp, Anthony, 137, 186
Campbell, 76, 153–4, 166
Carolingian dynasty, 140
Castille and Leon, Kings of, 141
Catuvellauni, Kings of, 161, 174, 178–80
Chancery records, 97, 103, 107–8, 112
Chang, Joseph T., 9
changes of name, 37–8, 153
Charlemagne, emperor, 52, 130, 136

mL 7-14